Study Guide to Accompany

From Slavery to Freedom

A History of African Americans

SEVENTH EDITION

Alfred A. Moss, Jr.
University of Maryland

Christopher Meagher

McGraw-Hill, Inc.

New York St. Louis San Francisco Auckland Bogotá
Caracas Lisbon London Madrid Mexico City Milan Montreal
New Delhi San Juan Singapore Sydney
Tokyo Toronto

Study Guide to Accompany

From
Slavery
to Freedom

A History of African Americans

This book is printed on acid-free paper.

5 6 7 8 9 0 DOC DOC 9 0 9 8 7

ISBN 0-07-021908-7

The editor was Peter Labella;
the production supervisor was Friederich W. Schulte.
R. R. Donnelley & Sons Company was printer and binder.

Table of Contents

Preface

This study guide was prepared to assist students with their reading of *From Slavery to Freedom*, Seventh Edition. Each of the twenty-four chapters contains a brief chronology, a chapter summary, chapter review questions, identifications, and a self-test section.

These different sections of the study guide can be used in a variety of ways, depending on both your needs and the requirements of your class. We suggest that you initially read the chapter summaries of this study guide in order to familiarize yourself with the most prominent themes and developments discussed in each chapter of the textbook. Next, read the chapter assigned by your teacher. After you have completed an initial reading, the study guide questions and identifications will help you to focus on some of the more significant facts and developments of African-American history. Once you've completed these steps, test your comprehension by answering the self-test questions.

You will soon discover that some of the chapters of this review guide are considerably longer than others. This is a function of two factors: first, certain periods of African-American history have had greater and more enduring significance to the lives of both black and white Americans than have others. The Civil War, Reconstruction, and the post-World War II Civil Rights Movement are three such examples. Secondly, from 1865 until the 1960s the literacy rate of African Americans expanded exponentially. Concomitant with this was the expansion of written records and of popular and scholarly studies of race relations in the United States; both developments allowed for a far richer understanding of the complexities of African-American life, and this helps explain why more recent African-American history is amply detailed.

We hope that your studies of African-American history will enable you to apprehend both the tragedies and triumphs, as well as the privations and pride, that have shaped the character of Americans of African descent living in the United States today.

Christopher Meagher

Alfred Moss

December 1993

Chapter I

Land of Their Ancestors

KEY EVENTS

1062	Reign of Ghana's Tenkamenin began
1076	Muslim Almoravids invaded Ghana
1235	Mali (Melle) began as an organized Kingdom
1312	Reign of Mansa-Musa began in Mali
1469	Songhay ruler Sonni Ali captured Timbuktu
1493	Askia Mohammed became ruler of Songhay

CHAPTER OVERVIEW

From the 7th century A.D. until the 16th century several powerful African states evolved. Of central importance were the nations of Ghana, Mali, and Songhay. These powerful kingdoms, like many other African states, were influenced to some degree by Islamic traditions and institutions; likewise, each kingdom influenced both the Arab people and other African people to the north, east, and south.

REVIEW QUESTIONS

Chapter Content Review

1. What was the first West African state of which there is any record? What other major states arose in this region?

2. What was the chief town/commercial center of Ghana during the Middle Ages?

3. What non-African group first entered West Africa around the 10th century? What religion did they introduce?

4. What products did Ghana exchange for the Muslim textiles, salt, brass, pearls, and other products?

5. Who was Tenkamenin? What type of authority did he have?

6. Explain the reasons for the decline of the kingdom of Ghana from the 11th to the 13th centuries?

7. What was a mansa? Which dynasty ruled Mali during the 13th and 14th centuries? Who was Sundiata Keita?

8. What contributions did Mansa-Musa and his successors make to the nation of Mali?

9. Who was Sonni Ali? By what means was Sonni Ali able to subdue the entire Niger region?

10. Why was Sonni Ali's reign over the Kingdom of Songhay filled with fighting?

11. Who was Askia Mohammed? How did he improve his empire?

12. What was the cultural significance of Timbuktu and Jenne?

13. What enabled the empire of Wagadugu (the Mossi states) to survive from about the 11th century until the 19th century?

Identification Questions

You should be able to describe the following key terms, concepts, individuals and places, and explain their significance:

1. Sisse dynasty
2. mansas
3. Suleiman
4. Askia Mohammed
5. Timbuktu
6. Mossi States
7. Benin
8. Yoruba
9. Empire of the Congo

Essay Questions

1. Explain why European people prior to the eighteenth century would view Africa as the "dark continent." Given the political cultures of the West African states of Ghana, Mali, and Songhay, is this view accurate?

2. Discuss the impact of Islam on the African states after 10th century.

SELF-TEST

Multiple Choice

1. The first West African state, according to existing records, was:
   a. Ghana
   b. Mali
   c. Zanzibar
   d. Songhay

2. The commercial center and chief town of the Ghanans during the Middle Ages was :
   a. Kumbi Saleh
   b. Timbuctu
   c. Wagadu
   d. Bambuhu

3. The first non-African cultural group to influence Ghana was:
   a. Greek
   b. Arab
   c. Hindu
   d. Roman

4. What legendary figure was credited with consolidating and strengthening the Kingdom of Mali in the 13th century?
   a. Sundiata Keita
   b. Mansa-Musa
   c. Tenkamenin

True/False

5. The first major West African state in recorded history was Songhay.

6. The legendary Malian leader credited with consolidating and strengthening the Kingdom of Mali was Sundiata Keita.

7. One of the chief Ghanan exports during the Sisse dynasty was gold.

8. Slavery did not exist in western Africa prior to the arrival of Europeans.

9. The mansa of Mali was the king.

10. The West African people of Mali, Songhay, and Ghana were heavily influenced by Christianity.

Chapter II

The African Way of Life

KEY EVENTS

1076	Muslim Almoravids invade Ghana
1235	Mali (Melle) begins as an organized Kingdom
1312	Reign of Mansa-Musa begins in Mali
1400s	Oral traditions of Africa recorded in Arabic
1469	Songhay ruler Sonni Ali captures Timbuktu
1493	Askia Mohammed becomes ruler of Songhay
1500-1800	African cultural forms transplanted to the New World
	Tarikh-es Soudan, a history of Sudan, is written by Es-Sadi.
	Tarikh-El-Fettach, written by Kati, a Sudanese.

CHAPTER OVERVIEW

On the eve of the sixteenth century Africa teemed with a rich diversity of cultures. Across the continent could be found stable political structures, diversified economies, and cohesive social institutions. Whether the states were great empires or modest political entities, they were generally well-organized and able to maintain law, order, and social harmony. This political stability both within and among the African states was conducive to healthy economic development. The Africans, whether farmers or artisans, displayed remarkable versatility and varieties of talents and tastes.

Most impressive in considering the social institutions of Africa was the cohesive influence of the family. The immediate family, the clan, and the tribe undergirded every aspect of life. The influence and hold the patriarch had over the members of the family was largely responsible for the stability which was characteristic of the area. The deep loyalty and attachment of the individual to the family approached reverence, and indeed, was the basis for most religious practices. Thus the world "discovered" by the fifteenth century Europeans was already highly civilized.

REVIEW QUESTIONS

Chapter Content Review

1. From which area of Africa did the vast majority of slaves originate?

2. What were the essential characteristics of the African village states?

3. What economic activities were common in Africa? What impact did commerce have on Africa?

4. Was Africa polygamist, monogamist, or a combination of both? What was usually the determining factor?

5. What was the basis for most social stratification in Africa?

6. Which Africans were or became slaves in Africa? Did the children of slaves have any rights?

7. Before the arrival of Islam what was the most common form of African religion? What religious rituals did the Africans practice?

8. Where did Islam have its greatest success on the African continent?

9. What impeded the spread of Islam and Christianity to central and Western Africa?

10. What inhibited the development of literary forms in Africa?

11. By what means were the multitude of African stories, histories and myths transmitted to later generations, both before and after the Moslem incursion?

12. What significance did the family have in the African social structure?

Identification Questions

You should be able to describe the following key terms, concepts, individuals and places, and explain their significance:

1. clan
2. ancestor worship
3. Suto/Ruanda/Banda
4. Es-Sadi and Kati
5. drum/guitar/zither

Essay Questions

1. Discuss the political, economic, and social structures of African life that the observant European trader or missionary would have encountered in the 16th century.

2. In what ways were the political, economic, and social structures of 13th to 16th century Africa similar to those of late medieval and early modern Europe.

SELF-TEST

Multiple Choice

1. In early African society, the eldest male was:
    a. usually the head of the family
    b. always the head of the family
    c. never the head of the family
    d. only rarely the head of the family

2. The practice of polygamy in early Africa was:
    a. forbidden
    b. denied to the converts of Islam
    c. permitted in virtually every region
    d. encouraged by Christian missionaries

3. The monarchs of West African political units were:
    a. rarely absolute rulers
    b. elected on the basis of universal manhood suffrage
    c. seldom, if ever, limited in their power
    d. always the eldest son of the royal family

Fill in the Blank

4. The _____ was the most basic unit of social organization in early Africa.

5. The most common form of government in the early African societies was _____.

6. The most common form of religion in early Africa was

_____.

True/False

7. Africans were neither primarily nomadic nor simply agricultural.

8. The use of iron developed very early in African economies.

9. The need for a cheap domestic labor force accounts for the practice of slavery in Africa.

10. The African clan or enlarged family was composed of all families that claimed a common ancestor.

Chapter III

The Slave Trade and the New World

KEY EVENTS

1300s   Commercial Revolution begins

1390   African slaves brought to Europe

1493   Pope Alexander VI creates demarcation line dividing the non-European world between Spain and Portugal

1517   Bartolemeo de Las Casas advocates encouragement of African immigration to the New World

1520s   Estevanico explores New Mexico and Arizona for the Spanish

1619   First African indentures sold in the Virginia colony

1640s   Rise of West Indian sugar plantations

1672   Royal African Company chartered by the King of England

CHAPTER OVERVIEW

Although the institution of slavery had existed for millennia and in a diversity of regions, it attained its brutal apex after the dawn of the European Commercial Revolution. Beginning in the fifteenth and sixteenth centuries Portuguese and Spanish sea-farers established prosperous trading posts along the coast of West Africa. In addition to the spices, gold, ivory, and agricultural products available, the Iberians perceived the potential of African slaves as surrogates for the decimated Indian laborers in the New World. By the seventeenth century the Spanish had created an American empire, heavily dependent on this slave labor.

Spanish dominance of the West Indies ended with the encroachments of Denmark, Britain, France, and the Netherlands upon the Spanish slave trade monopoly. These other nations eventually competed vigorously for the profits derived from both the slave trade and the fruits of West Indian slave labor: tobacco, indigo, and cotton. After 1640, the substantial profits derived from the sugar plantations engendered a virtual flooding of the West Indies with African slaves. Throughout this region the institution of slavery varied depending on time, ratio of slaves to whites, cost of slaves and market price for a given crop, and other factors. Yet in all regions of the Americas slavery represented abject and inhuman cruelty.

REVIEW QUESTIONS

Chapter Content Review

1. In what capacity did the Islamic political and economic elites use African slaves?

2. In what ways did the Renaissance and the Commercial Revolution in Europe create the modern system of slavery and the slave trade?

3. Which European countries during the 15th century created the foundation for the African slave trade of later years? How did they justify their actions?

4. Where did Africans play significant roles in the process of exploring and discovering America?

5. Why was Indian slavery in the New World unprofitable?

6. Why did white indentured servitude prove unsatisfactory?

7. What advantages were there in resorting to African labor in the American colonies?

8. By the 18th century which nation had clearly emerged as the dominant slave trader?

9. In what ways did the introduction of European weaponry influence the future of Western Africa?

10. In what region of the New World was the first complement of slaves sent? Why were they sent there?

11. Which European countries broke the Spanish monopoly of the slave trade in the West Indies in both the 16th and 17th centuries?

12. What were the consequences of the Dutch proposal that the West Indies planters begin growing sugar cane?

13. For what reason did the planters of the West Indies overpopulate their plantations with slaves?

14. What effect did absentee landlordism have on typical slave living conditions in the West Indies?

15. Describe the diet and the working conditions typical for West Indian slaves.

16. What factors led to the increase in exportation of slaves from the West Indies to the American mainland?

17. In what economic pursuits were Brazilian slaves employed?

Identification Questions

You should be able to describe the following key terms, concepts, individuals and places, and explain their significance:

1. Estevanico
2. Negroes de Gano
3. Bartolomeo De Las Casas
4. caboceer
5. "middle passage"
6. absentee landlordism
7. seasoning process
8. Maroons
9. Macandal
10. asiento
11. Viceroyalty of New Granada
12. mestizos
13. Jean Baptiste Point du Sable

Essay Questions

1. In what ways did eighteenth and nineteenth century Latin American slavery differ from slavery on the British mainland?

2. What affects did the slave trade have on West Africa and the future of African civilizations?

SELF-TEST

Multiple Choice

1. Important to the slave-trade was
    a. the active cooperation of certain African chiefs
    b. the desire of large numbers of Africans to migrate to the West Indies
    c. the friendly relationship between Christian missionaries and Muslims
    d. the convenient overland route between West and North Africa

2. According to Professor Philip D. Curtin, the total number of slaves imported to the New World between 1451 and 1870 was (approximately):
    a. 1,340,000
    b. 6,050,000
    c. 9,600,000
    d. 1,900,000

3. Plantation slaves in the West Indies were:
    a. most often supervised directly by their owners
    b. engaged primarily in the cultivation of cotton
    c. generally left in the hands of overseers whose chief concern was to produce wealth for their employers
    d. seldom discontented with their lot

Fill in the Blank

4. Runaway slaves in places like Haiti or Jamaica were called

    _____.

5. _____ referred to the process of "breaking-in" newcomers to the islands' slave population.

6. _____ were Europeans who, in exchange for their passage to the New World, voluntarily sold their labor for a specified period of time.

7. _____ was the black explorer who is credited with opening New Mexico and Arizona for the Spaniards.

True/False

8. Of all European nations, Portugal realized the greatest profits from the slave trade.

9. Africans were first used in the West Indies to cultivate sugar cane.

10. Africans offered stiff resistance to their capture, sale, and transportation to the New World.

Chapter IV

Colonial Slavery

KEY EVENTS

CHAPTER OVERVIEW

In 1619, the first Africans transported to the mainland British American colonies were received as indentured servants. Over the next fifty years the status of their descendants and other Africans in the Chesapeake colonies would diminish to the level of chattel slaves. Like slavery in the West Indies, British colonial slavery proved to be a convenient substitute for white and Indian labor along the southern Atlantic coast. In Virginia and Maryland, successful subjugation of the Africans, coupled with increasing agricultural wealth, stimulated the expansion of slavery into the Carolinas and Georgia, especially after 1700.

Slavery was introduced to the Middle Colonies and New England in the first half of the 17th century. Yet unlike the South, where large slave populations engendered extensive fears of rebellion, slaves and free blacks constituted only a small fraction of the population.

REVIEW QUESTIONS

Chapter Content Review

1. What was the legal status of most Africans who landed in the Virginia colony prior to 1650?

2. What accounts for the decline of the Africans' status in the Chesapeake region in the mid-seventeen century and thereafter? What were some of the aspects of Virginia's slave code and why was it so harsh?

3. Was the institution of slavery as it evolved in Maryland significantly different from that of Virginia?

4. Were the Carolinas originally planned as a slave colony? Explain.

5. Why did South Carolina have the most stringent slave code found in the British colonies?

6. What impact did the Quakers have on the institution of slavery in North Carolina?

7. How pervasive was slavery in the British North American colonies from 1680-1750? In which of the Middle Atlantic colonies did the largest number of slaves reside?

8. Why was slavery unsuccessful in the Middle Colonies?

9. Why were the New England slave codes that developed less stringent than the codes of other colonies.

Identification Questions

You should be able to describe the following key terms, concepts, individuals and places, and explain their significance:

1. Society for the Propagation of the Gospel in Foreign Parts
2. Stono Rebellion
3. slave codes
4. Society of Friends (Quakers)
5. Fundamental (of the Carolinas)

Essay Questions

1. Compare and contrast the forms of slavery that emerged in the Caribbean islands and the British American colonies north of Florida.

2. The settlers of the New World were overwhelmingly Christian people who felt duty bound to obey the laws of God. How could they have been both God-fearing Christians and participants in a slaving society?

SELF-TEST

Multiple Choice

1. The twenty blacks who were brought to Jamestown in 1619:
   a. were immediately deported
   b. were slaves under existing Virginia law
   c. were "seasoned" and then sent to the West Indies
   d. occupied a position similar to that of the white indentures

2. Three of the following answers concerning colonial slave codes are false. Which one is true?
   a. They provided the method by which masters could easily manumit slaves
   b. They safeguarded the civil and political rights of slaves.
   c. They were regulatory in nature and designed to suppress rebellion and control conduct
   d. They generally permitted slaves freedom of movement and freedom of assembly

3. During the Colonial Period slavery was a legal institution:
   a. only in the South
   b. in all thirteen colonies
   c. only in the middle colonies
   d. in the southern and middle colonies, but not in New England

Fill in the Blank

4. The landing of blacks in the _____ colony marked the beginning of the forced importation of black people into the North American mainland.

5. The _____ were a religious group largely responsible for the comparatively slow growth of slavery in Pennsylvania.

6. _____ This region's primary interest in slavery came through the slave trade.

7. _____ Two dramatic slave rebellions took place in this middle colony in the seventeenth century.

True/False

8. At the time it was founded slavery was banned in the Carolinas.

9. Statutory recognition of slavery in Virginia did not come until 1661.

10. The relations between colonial Virginia and colonial Maryland in the 18th century were strained because Virginia's slaves could escape easily to Maryland where slavery was illegal.

Chapter V

That All May Be Free

KEY EVENTS

1763   French-Indian War ends

1764   Sugar Act

1770   Boston Massacre; Crispus Attucks slain

1775   Quakers organize first antislavery society

Lord Dunsmore offers emancipation to those slaves who would fight the colonials

1776   Declaration of Independence signed

Policy of excluding blacks from the Continental Army is repealed

1787   Northwest Ordinance bans slavery in territory north of the Ohio River

Constitutional Convention

CHAPTER OVERVIEW

By the end of the French-Indian War slavery had become both a commonly accepted and an integral part of the colonial American economy. Although heavily concentrated in the Southern colonies, slavery benefited northern commercial interests. The French-Indian War, however, exposed the growing conflict between colonial economic and British imperial objectives. This conflict culminated in the British imposition of stringent economic controls on the colonials. Moreover, this assertion of arbitrary power engendered the American Revolution. The Revolution was a political, ideological, and armed struggle between the British and the British American colonials, replete with passion over the notions of liberty, property, equality, and slavery.

The American Revolutionary Period of 1763-1776 saw the emergence of a broad-based antislavery movement. Yet the antislavery movement at this time was fueled more by anti-British sentiment than by passionate commitment to the ideals of human liberty and equality. Despite the efforts of fervent Quakers and a multitude of antislavery societies during and after the years of the War for Independence, the forces of political compromise and conservatism would prevail at the nation's historic Constitutional Convention of 1787. Among the values of life, liberty and property, property emerged preeminent; and the liberty of white men to possess as property black men was established as a first principle of the Republic.

REVIEW QUESTIONS

Chapter Content Review

1. How did the end of the French-Indian War usher in a new approach to the problem of slavery in the British-American colonies?

2. How did the British contribute to the growth of the anti-slavery movement?

3. What impact did American revolutionary ferment have on blacks in the mid-Atlantic and New England colonies?

4. Whom does Jefferson blame for the continuation of the slave trade in America (in the "Summary View of the Rights of British America")?

5. Why were the colonists increasingly willing to prohibit the importation of slaves from 1774 to 1776?

6. Explain why the colonials were or were not willing to prohibit the importation of slaves after 1776.

7. Were blacks a part of the early revolutionary military efforts in Massachusetts?

8. What factors compelled George Washington to reconsider his decision to prohibit the recruitment of blacks for the Continental Army?

9. During the Revolutionary War what impact did British occupation of slaveholding areas have on the institution of slavery?

10. What effect did the Revolutionary War have on slavery?

11. What benefits did the War bring some slaves?

12. For what reasons did states refuse to permit enlistments by blacks?

13. How did the all-black units of the Continental Army fare in battle?

14. Why did South Carolina, but not Virginia, object so vigorously to the proposed abolition of the slave trade?

15. Did the Constitution sanction the slave trade?

Identification Questions

You should be able to describe the following key terms, concepts, individuals and places, and explain their significance:

1. Crispus Attucks
2. Summary View of the Rights of British America
3. Lord John Murray Dunmore
4. Northwest Ordinance
5. Three-fifths Compromise

Essay Questions

1. What social implications did the Revolutionary ideas contain and how did these ideas influence state legislatures in the post war years?

2. What impact was the Revolutionary War likely to have on blacks who served in the patriots' cause? In what way would the black soldier view the war differently from the white soldier?

SELF-TEST

Multiple Choice

1. One passage of the original draft of the Declaration of Independence that Jefferson was persuaded to omit :
   a. declared all slaves free
   b. upheld the king's right to rule the colonies
   c. condemned slavery
   d. asserted that all men were created equal

2. All of the following were black soldiers who distinguished themselves in battle except:
   a. Edward Rutledge
   b. Prince Hall
   c. Peter Salem
   d. Salem Poor

3. The Three-Fifths Compromise of the Constitution:
   a. reconciled the interests of creditors and debtors
   b. protected the African slave trade for a time
   c. stipulated that fugitive slaves be returned to masters
   d. provided for the counting of slaves for the purposes of representation in Congress and taxation

Fill in the Blank

4. One of the two states opposed to the enlistment of black soldiers throughout the Revolutionary War was _____.

5. The Royal Governor of Virginia who offered freedom to slaves in return for service to the British army was _____.

6. The British policy of benign or salutary neglect came to an end with the conclusion of the _____ war in 1763.

True/False

7. Since the bulk of the black population was in the South, the majority of black soldiers in the patriot armies came from this section.

8. The vast majority of black soldiers served in primarily white units during the Revolutionary War.

9. There are many instances of blacks serving in the Revolutionary navy during the War for Independence.

10. Manumission and antislavery societies became more numerous after the Revolutionary War.

Chapter VI

Blacks in the New Republic

KEY EVENTS

1787	Free African Society organized
1789	French Revolution commences
1791	Benjamin Banneker publishes his first almanac
1791-1801	Rebellion of Santo Domingan slaves
1793	Cotton gin invented
	Congress enacts Fugitive Slave Law.
1800	Toussaint L'Ouverture captured
1803	Louisiana Purchase
1807	Congress enacts ban on the importation of slaves

CHAPTER OVERVIEW

By the last decade of the nineteenth century some four million people inhabited the United States. 750,000 of these people were of African descent and of these approximately 700,000 were owned by other human beings. Although slavery was gradually undergoing a process of obsolescence in the North at the turn of the century, the incessant lure of western land and effects of the Industrial Revolution would consign the great multitude of these "children of Africa" and their progeny to sixty more years of chattel slavery.

With the introduction of the cotton gin, new life was breathed into American slavery. The gin permitted an enormous expansion of cotton agriculture; coupled with the seemingly insatiable demand of British textile manufacturers, the need for field hands increased exponentially. Lured by high cotton prices, thousands rushed to secure land in the rich soils of the American southwest. With an increasing demand for cotton laborers the domestic slave trade burgeoned, and American participation in the international slave trade continued: legally before 1808 and illicitly there after. Slavery and the slave trade had become, by the early nineteenth century, an important cog in the wheel of American economic progress.

Simultaneous with the entrenchment of slavery evolved the commitment of free blacks to create their own social, religious, and educational institutions for the purposes of achieving a greater degree of independence, pride, and fulfillment. Black scientists, poets, writers, teachers, preachers, and abolitionists all struggled to both advance the cause of independence for black Americans and to advance the intellectual, moral, and spiritual life of America.

REVIEW QUESTIONS

Chapter Content Review

1. Which state had the greatest number of slaves in 1790?

2. What twin evils plagued the post-Revolutionary War tobacco plantations?

3. What revolutionary advances in technology would contribute to the sustenance of African slavery in America at the end of the eighteenth century?

4. What made the transition from rice, indigo, or tobacco farming to cotton farming so easy?

5. What role did New England merchants play in this movement toward cotton agriculture?

6. How did the Southern states respond to the news of slave revolution in the West Indies beginning in 1791?

7. What relevance did the government's purchase of Louisiana have on slavery in the United States?

8. In 1807 the United States outlawed the slave trade. What impact did this legislation have?

9. What groups in America established the first schools for blacks?

10. What inhibited the development of schools for blacks in Virginia and the Carolinas around 1800?

11. What factors contributed to the development of racially separate churches in America?

12. What checked the growth of "Negro Methodism" in the South in the early 19th century?

13. What opportunities did segregated worship provide for American blacks?

Identification Questions

You should be able to describe the following key terms, concepts, individuals and places, and explain their significance:

1. Eli Whitney
2. Toussaint L'Ouverture
3. General Le Clerc
4. Fugitive Slave Act of 1793
5. Stephen R. Bradley
6. Jupiter Hammon
7. Phillis Wheatley
8. Gustavus Vassa
9. Benjamin Banneker
10. James Derham
11. Paul Cuffe
12. Andrew Bryan
13. Richard Allen

Essay Questions

1. In what ways did segregation serve the interests of American blacks at the turn of the century? Focus on both developments in the West Indies and religious developments in the United States around the turn of the century.

2. The resiliency and the adaptability of African Americans is amply demonstrated by black cultural achievements at the turn of the century. Explain.

SELF-TEST

Multiple Choice

1. The black population of the new United States in 1790
   a. was concentrated in cities and towns
   b. was essentially rural
   c. included no free black men and women
   d. numbered more than one million

2. According to the census of 1790, the vast majority of blacks lived in the South Atlantic states. Where were blacks most numerous?
   a. Georgia
   b. South Carolina
   c. Virginia
   d. Maryland

3. An accomplished black man who was editor of almanacs and who served on the commission appointed to define the boundaries and lay out the streets of the District of Columbia was:
   a. Prince Hall
   b. Benjamin Banneker
   c. Paul Cuffe
   d. Richard Allen

Fill in the Blank

4. One of the only states that reported no slaves in its population in 1790 was _____.

5. _____ was the inventor of the cotton gin.

6. The black leader of antislavery forces in Haiti who successfully overthrew French rule on that island was _____.

7. _____ was the founder of Bethel Church in Philadelphia, the first African Methodist Church in the United States.

True/False

8. In the years immediately following the Revolutionary War, there was some reason to believe that slavery would deteriorate.

9. Revolutionary activity in the Caribbean at the turn of the century had little effect on the course of United States history.

10. The federal law banning the slave trade was rigidly enforced after 1808.

Chapter VII

Blacks and Manifest Destiny

KEY EVENTS

1803   Louisiana Purchase

1803-1806   Lewis and Clark expedition

1812   Louisiana enters the Union as the eighteenth state

           War with Great Britain commences

1814   Treaty of Ghent signed: war concludes

1817   Mississippi enters the Union as the twentieth state

1819   Alabama enters the Union as the twenty-second state

1820   Missouri Compromise; Missouri enters the Union as the twenty-fourth state

CHAPTER OVERVIEW

The initial years of the nineteenth century provided citizens of the United States with ample reason for optimism. Land was cheap and plentiful, and with the acquisition of the Louisiana territory, farming soil seemed virtually limitless. The cost of these frontier blessings and the concomitant expansion of white liberty and democracy, however, would be borne by the black race in America. To areas south of the Ohio River, and especially to the rich soils of the southwest territories, slave traders rushed their commodities to bolster the newly created cotton kingdom. Between 1812 and 1820 four slave states were added to the union.

Expansionism had other costs. Aggressive expansionists from the western and southern states of America contributed in large measure to the outbreak of war with Great Britain in 1812. While the war was economically disastrous for the young American economy, it provided the opportunity for many blacks to obtain their freedom. As in the Revolutionary War, blacks served the United States with valor and distinction. With the conclusion of the war came an acceleration of western migration and the expansion of slavery. Prices for field hands doubled in some areas after the war, thus prompting both the expansion of America's illegal slave imports and southern calls to repeal the 1807 ban on the foreign slave trade. Clearly the emergent theories of "manifest destiny" had different connotations for blacks and whites in America.

REVIEW QUESTIONS

Chapter Content Review

1. What forces rendered resistance to the encroaching forces of slavery futile?

2. What contributions did black Americans like York, Edward Rose, and Pierre Bonga make to the settlement of the American West?

3. Why did the American "warhawks" expect that war with Great Britain would advance or extend slavery?

4. What contributions did blacks make to the 1812 War effort?

5. What factors accounted for the great emigration of Southerners to the west during the first third of the 19th century?

6. What relevance did Texas have to the lords of the Cotton Kingdom during the first half of the 19th century?

7. What effect did the interstate trafficking of slaves have on antislavery sentiment in Maryland and Virginia?

8. What impact did the 1807 ban on the importation of African slaves have on American slaving interests ?

9. For what reasons might a slave owner hire out or lease his slaves?

10. For what reason would an individual who owned no slaves hire a slave from a slave-owner instead of purchasing one?

11. What competition did America's interstate slave traders face in the first half of the nineteenth century?

12. Why did the states of the upper South reject calls to reopen the slave trade?

Identification Questions

You should be able to describe the following key terms, concepts, individuals and places, and explain their significance:

1. James Beckwourth
2. Edmonia Lewis
3. war hawks
4. Treaty of Ghent
5. Manifest Destiny
6. slave breeding

Essay Questions

1. Despite numerous geographical and economic differences, the various parts of the South developed into an economically united section of the United States. Explain the reasons for this.

2. The slave trader had a more profound effect on the history of the Southern frontier than did the Indian trader." Defend or dispute this assertion.

SELF-TEST

Multiple Choice

1. One of the causes of the War of 1812 was:
    a. British efforts to end the slave trade
    b. the desire of some American leaders to acquire more territory
    c. the failure to resolve a boundary dispute between the United States and British Canada
    d. the attempt on Britain's part to regain American lands lost in the Revolution

2. This was called the "very seat and center of the slave trade."
    a. Charleston
    b. Memphis
    c. the District of Columbia
    d. New Orleans

3. Which of the following represented the attempt to secure a supply of labor for work in the cotton kingdom?
    a. establishment of the domestic slave trade
    b. illegal importation of slaves from Africa
    c. both a and b
    d. neither a or b

Fill in the Blank

4. _____ was described as "the most intrepid and re-markable of the black explorers of the American West."

5. _____ were those members of Congress representing southern and western states who advocated war with Britain in 1812.

6. The _____ was the 1787 statute that prohibited slavery in the territory north of the Ohio River.

True/False

7. There is no record of blacks participating in the exploration of the trans-Mississippi West.

8. One of the most important factors augmenting the westward movement was the domestic slave trade.

9. Blacks served in the army but not in the navy in the War of 1812.

10. The extension of democracy was not the primary motive of the southern expansionists.

Chapter VIII

That Peculiar Institution

KEY EVENTS

1790   Slave population of the United States circa 690,000

1800   Gabriel Prosser leads a slave insurrection in Virginia

1822   Denmark Vesey's planned slave insurrection is thwarted in South Carolina

1830   Slave population of the United States circa 2,100,000

1831   Nat Turner leads a slave revolt in Southampton County, Virginia

CHAPTER OVERVIEW

In the first half of the nineteenth century, slavery expanded throughout the South and served as the basis for the expansion of southern wealth and production. At the same time slavery exerted increasing influence on the course of the South's social and political developments. As cotton cultivators, the slaves served as the essential means for accumulating wealth; as capital, they were the most important form of southern wealth. But this "capital" was of a peculiar nature. As human beings held in bondage and deprived of the fruits of their labor, the slave-capital required careful motivating and supervision. From these circumstances emerged the essentials of a "peculiar" institution and the peculiar southern society of the Antebellum Period.

Rooted in agrarianism and the expansion of its staples (cotton, rice, tobacco, and sugar cane), southern society was led by the wealthy planter class. Comprising less than two percent of the white families, planters nevertheless exerted dominant influence over the course of southern economics, politics, and culture. Of primary concern to the planters and lesser slaveholders of the South was the preservation of the status quo. To control the slaves and to induce them to produce bounteous crops, rigid laws and systems of control were devised. The slave codes, community patrols, religious indoctrination, threats, and forms of torture were essential elements of the peculiar institution. Not surprisingly, insurrection was the greatest of the fears of southern white citizenry. Although only twenty-five percent of these people owned slaves, all citizens had an abiding interest in preserving the slave system.

Black resistance to slavery was both persistent and omnipresent in the south. Whether simply breaking a tool or fleeing captivity, the slaves never fully accepted their status. Through song, stories, dance, religion and familial ties, slaves created for themselves meaningful community in which their dignity was affirmed.

REVIEW QUESTIONS

Chapter Content Review

1. What was the size of the slave population of the United States on the eve of the Civil War? What was the size of the southern white population?

2. How did slavery shape the social structure of the South and dominate the political and economic thinking of Southerners?

3. For what purposes were the slave codes created? What did they prohibit?

4. By what means were slave codes enforced?

5. How many acres of cotton could a single slave typically plant, cultivate, and harvest in a single year?

6. Why were slaves directed by an overseer more likely to receive crueler treatment than slaves under the direction of the plantation owner?

7. How many slaves lived in urban communities in 1850? In what type of work were they engaged?

8. In what types of recreational activities did plantation slaves frequently engage?

9. Why did slaveowners frequently demand slave attendance at Christian services held at white churches?

10. Why did many planters fear slave piety?

11. What impact did the illegal schools for southern blacks have after the Civil War?

12. What obstacles prevented slaves from forming stable family units?

13. What percentage of the slave population was visibly mulatto in 1850?

14. What types of legal restrictions prevented cruel or inhuman treatment toward the slave?

15. What form of Negro resistance to slavery did white communities fear most?

Identification Questions

You should be able to describe the following key terms, concepts, individuals and places, and explain their significance:

1. Slave Codes
2. patrols
3. vigilance committees
4. field hand
5. house servant
6. Henry Blair
7. Benjamin Montgomery
8. John Canoe celebration
9. Gabriel Prosser
10. Denmark Vesey
11. Nat Turner

Essay Questions

1. If you had to make the unenviable choice of living as field hand (slave) or a house servant (slave), which would it be? Why? What advantages/disadvantages do you see in each?

2. Commonly heard among the planter class were accusations that their slaves were guilty of delinquency, thievery, sloth, and aversion to "civilizing" tendencies. What aspects of slave life may have contributed to the formulation of these accusations?

SELF-TEST

Multiple Choice

1. In 1860, three-fourths of the white people of the South:
    a. owned twenty or more slaves
    b. had neither slaves nor an immediate economic interest in the maintenance of slavery
    c. were operators of large plantations
    d. favored the immediate abolition of slavery

2. Slave codes expressed the point of view that:
   a. slaves were not persons but property
   b. laws should protect the ownership of slave property
   c. whites should be protected against possible slave rebellion
   d. all of the above

3. It was generally believed that:
   a. one slave was required for the cultivation of three acres of cotton
   b. each slave should be given a specific work assignment or task each day
   c. house servants were more valuable than field hands
   d. slaves should never be exposed to any form of religious activity

Fill in the Blank

4. Although a distinct minority in southern society, the _____ were that class that exercised a disproportionate amount of influence.

5. The _____ was an adoption of the militia in the south used to maintain slavery. It functioned to enforce the slave codes in communities.

6. Plantation slaves labored generally under the "task" or "gang" system. Under which did the majority work? _____

True/False

7. A majority of southern whites owned slaves.

8. Slave owners generally selected their overseers from the slave-holding class.

9. Despite legal restrictions, some slaves were taught to read and write.

10. The southern church came to be used as an agency for maintaining slavery.

Chapter IX

Quasi-Free Negroes

KEY EVENTS

1790   59,000 free blacks in the United States

1810   Maryland repeals the right of black suffrage

1817   American Colonization Society is formed

1826   First blacks in America graduate from American colleges

1827   Freedman's Journal, the first African-American newspaper is published

1830   319,000 free blacks in the United States

1834   Tennessee repeals black suffrage laws

          African Methodist Episcopal Church begins publishing *The Christian Herald*

1853   Establishment of the National Council of Colored People

1860   488,000 free blacks in the United States

CHAPTER OVERVIEW

One peculiarity of the slave societies in the Antebellum south was the existence of "free blacks". Neither slave nor free, these descendants of manumitted people and ex-indentures lived at the fringe of southern society (except perhaps in the states of Maryland and Virginia) and lived as inconspicuously as possible. Because their status as non-slaves contradicted the cultural distinction of whites/free and blacks/slave, southern white legislatures imposed increasingly rigid restrictions on the quasi-free blacks to minimize the impact their "freedom" might have on their enslaved brethren.

North of the Mason-Dixon line, where slavery had been abolished, the free blacks also faced innumerable obstacles in securing for themselves the blessings conferred upon independent citizens. Usually denied political and social rights in the states and communities where they dwelled, and not infrequently the victims of rigid segregation and violent attacks, northern blacks responded by creating independent institutions: churches, newspapers, businesses, and social service networks which catered to their interests.

Whether from the north or the south, free blacks had few opportunities to enjoy the lands of the American west. Western states often prohibited black settlement within their borders. Free blacks who did settle west of the Appalachian Mountains faced the hostility of white communities, rampant discrimination, and requisite segregation. Not surprisingly, no small number of free blacks in the Antebellum Period found the notion of colonization in Africa appealing.

REVIEW QUESTIONS

Chapter Content Review

1. For what reasons did Southern masters manumit their slaves?

2. What factors, other than manumission, account for the increase in the number of free blacks in the South?

3. In what areas of the country were free blacks concentrated on the eve of the Civil War?

4. Why was the existence of free-blacks in the South so precarious?

5. What economic and legal restrictions were imposed on the free blacks in the south?

6. What became of black suffrage in America after the Revolutionary Era?

7. What impediments prevented free black tradespeople from enjoying economic liberty?

8. What accounted for the growth of black fraternal and benevolent institutions in urban centers prior to the Civil War?

9. What happened to the black Methodist and Baptist churches between 1820 and 1860?

10. How common was public education for blacks in the midwest prior to the Civil War?

11. What institutions of higher learning were created for blacks in the antebellum years?

12. Despite mob violence, rampant discrimination, and mandated segregation, free blacks in the North had a great advantage over Southern free blacks. Explain.

13. Where did the colonization approach to the "Negro problem" originate and what was Paul Cuffe's contribution to it?

14. For what reasons did the American Colonization Society fail?

Identification Questions

You should be able to describe the following key terms, concepts, individuals and places, and explain their significance:

1. Cyprian Ricard
2. Solomon Humphries
3. placage
4. The Christian Herald
5. Phoenix Societies
6. George Moses Horton
7. William Wells Brown
8. Freedom's Journal
9. North Star
10. National Council of Colored People

Essay Questions

1. Despite their status as legally free, "free" blacks were no better than bondsmen. Assess the validity of this assertion.

2. The history of the colonization movement is filled with examples of black disharmony. Explain why emigration from America was simultaneously applauded and scorned by different black groups within the United States.

SELF-TEST

Multiple Choice

1. Census figures reveal that this state had a larger population of free blacks than any other.
    a. Virginia
    b. Maryland
    c. Pennsylvania
    d. New York

2. Despite the organized effort to colonize free blacks, about only _____ migrated:
   a. 1,420
   b. 30,000
   c. 10,000
   d. 15,000

3. The first black newspaper published in the United States was:
   a. *Freedom's Journal*
   b. *North Star*
   c. *Colored Man's Journal*
   d. *Anglo-African*

Fill in the Blank

4. _____ was the legal status of children born to free mothers.

5. The _____ was the name of the newspaper first published by Frederick Douglass in 1847.

6. The _____ was an organization formed for the purpose of commencing the colonization of American blacks in Africa.

True/False

7. Some slaves were able to gain their freedom through self-purchase.

8. Manumission carried with it civil and political rights as well as legal freedom.

9. Their hatred of slavery explains the absence of slaveholding among free blacks.

10. Racial animosity in the North forced Negroes in that section to totally support colonization.

Chapter X

Slavery and Intersectional Strife

KEY EVENTS

1820   Missouri Compromise

1821   The Genius of Universal Emancipation first published

1829   David Walker's Appeal published

1831   The Liberator first published

New England Antislavery Society formed

1840   Liberty Party formed

1847   Frederick Douglass elected president of the New England Anti-Slavery Society

1850   Compromise of 1850

Fugitive Slave Act enacted

1852   *Uncle Tom's Cabin* first published

1854   Kansas-Nebraska Act Republican Party formed

1857   *Dred Scott v. Sanford* decision

1859   John Brown conducts raid on Harper's Ferry

1860   Republican Abraham Lincoln elected president

CHAPTER OVERVIEW

Costly though the War of 1812 was, it nevertheless contributed briefly to the formation of national unity and greater political cooperation among the states of the north and south. Yet the essential differences between the increasingly reformist and industrial North and the slave-dependent agrarian South created a wedge with the potential to divide the sections permanently. In 1819 two powerful American values, antislavery and expansionism, converged and clashed in the congressional deliberations over the fate of Missouri, which had sought admission to the union as the twelfth slave state. Compromise was the solution to the sectional breach in 1820, but the seeds of mutual distrust were planted.

Prior to the 1820s, religious antislavery and economic considerations had pressured slave owners either to improve the conditions of slavery, manumit slaves, or support the colonization movement. Gradually, however, the antislavery movement became increasingly strident and intolerant of the "peculiar" institution and those who maintained it. Abolitionists such as David Walker, William Lloyd Garrison, Frederick Douglass, and Theodore Weld infuriated white southerners with their publications. In response, some white southerners began to fashion an ideological defense of slavery and the southern way of life. Moreover, as the abolitionist attacks increased, white southerners closed ranks and flexed their political muscle. In 1836 southern congressmen were able to impose the "gag-rule" in Congress, preventing the reading of antislavery petitions sent to the House of Representatives. In the 1840s southern politicians successfully promoted the future expansion of slavery by securing the annexation of Texas and by winning the Mexican Cession lands via war.

Unlike the war of 1812, the Mexican War divided northerners and southerners and put an end to the national consensus regarding American expansionism. To northerners, expansionism had become synonymous with extending and perpetuating chattel slavery and this they wouldn't countenance. To southerners, the opportunity to cultivate soils in the west with the aid of their human property became a prerequisite for their continued cooperation in the union. Throughout the 1850s this conflict intensified. The Compromise of 1850, which was crafted by Congressional leaders to preserve national unity, proved completely inadequate to the task of resolving what had become a divisive, emotional, and moral issue to a majority of Americans. Popular sovereignty applied in Kansas, a strengthened fugitive slave law, and the Supreme Court's 1857 Dred Scott decision all exacerbated the sectional tensions they were intended to subdue.

Finally in 1859 an abolitionist by the name of John Brown demonstrated to the south how their peculiar institution might be destroyed, and shortly thereafter the sword replaced both the pen and politics as the means for resolving the sectional conflict.

REVIEW QUESTIONS

Chapter Content Review

1. Which individuals initiated the movement toward radical abolitionism in America?

2. How did the abolitionism of David Walker and William Lloyd Garrison differ?

3. With what other reform movements of the early eighteenth century were militant antislavery associated?

4. How did James Birney and Theodore Weld advance the cause of antislavery?

5. Why did Garrison split the American Anti-Slavery Society in the 1839?

6. How did the Liberty Party originate?

7. Which abolitionist tactic engendered the greatest opposition to abolitionism in America?

8. How active were blacks in the national anti-slavery organizations?

9. Why was Frederick Douglass so important to the anti-slavery movement?

10. Why was the Underground Railroad such a threat to sectional harmony after 1830?

11. Approximately how many slaves escaped via the Underground Railroad between 1810 and 1850?

12. What events in the early 1820s convinced the residents of the South that they had to give more attention to the defense of slavery?

13. Other than writing pamphlets, in what other activities did southern communities engage to limit abolitionism?

14. What groups in America were steadfast against the Compromise measures of 1850?

15. In what way did the Kansas-Nebraska Act of 1854 doom the Compromise of 1850?

16. What impact did the Dred Scott decision have on the anti-slavery movement?

17. What impact did John Brown's raid on Harper's Ferry have on the South?

18. Why was the South unalterably opposed to the Republican Party?

Identification Questions

You should be able to describe the following key terms, concepts, individuals and places, and explain their significance:

1. David Walker
2. Benjamin Lundy
3. William Lloyd Garrison
4. Charles Finney
5. Oberlin College
6. Lewis Tappan
7. American and Foreign Anti-Slavery Society
8. Elijah Lovejoy
9. gag rule
10. Joshua Giddings
11. Samuel Cornish
12. Freedom's Journal
13. Harriet Tubman
14. John Fairfield
15. Harriet Beecher Stowe
16. Kansas-Nebraska Act
17. John Brown

Essay Questions

1. What religious, ideological, economic, and cultural arguments were made against slavery in America?

2. What arguments did the defenders of slavery make to justify the institution?

3. The "Negro problem" was undoubtedly the single greatest issue confronting all Americans from 1812-1850. Explain what this "problem" involved and why it created such tension.

SELF-TEST

Multiple Choice

1. Which part of the compromise of 1850 did the South find most objectionable?
   a. the admission of California as a free state
   b. the provision that certain territories be organized without mention of slavery (i.e. organized according to popular sovereignty)
   c. a stringent fugitive slave law
   d. the abolition of the slave trade in the District of Columbia

2. Which of the following was not a major southern defense of slavery?
   a. black people were inferior and destined for a subordinate position in society
   b. the Bible sanctioned slavery
   c. slavery was unprofitable: if let alone would rapidly fade out
   d. slave labor was an economic necessity to the South

3. The election of 1860 brought to the presidency:
   a. one who advocated reopening the African slave trade
   b. an opponent of the further extension of slavery
   c. a man highly acceptable to southerners
   d. a militant abolitionist

Fill in the Blank

4. The _____ was organized in 1833 and its members were committed to a crusade for the immediate abolition of slavery.

5. The name given to the action of the House of Representatives that, from 1836 to 1845, denied Americans the right of petition was the _____.

6. The _____ was an organized effort to undermine slavery by assisting runaway slaves escaping from the South.

True/False

7. Militant abolitionists supported the idea of financial compensation to owners of freed slaves.

8. Militant abolitionists were, on the whole, opposed to colonization.

9. Black men spoke out in favor of emancipation but were not permitted to support it in print.

10. Lincoln won the election of 1860 primarily because of his substantial electoral vote from the south.

Chapter XI

The Civil War

KEY EVENTS

1861   (February) South Carolina, Mississippi, Florida, Alabama, Georgia, and Louisiana secede from the union. They convene and adopt a provisional constitution for the Confederate States of America

(March) Lincoln is inaugurated

(April) Civil War begins as Fort Sumter is taken by South Carolina

(May) Texas, Arkansas, Tennessee, Virginia, and North Carolina secede

1862   (April) Slaves emancipated in the District of Columbia

(July) South Carolinian "Negro Regiment" activated

(September) Preliminary Emancipation Proclamation issued

1863   (January) Emancipation Proclamation issued

(July) Union troops defeat Confederates at Gettysburg

1864   Sherman's March to the Sea

1865   General Robert E. Lee surrenders at Appomattox; Civil
War ends

CHAPTER OVERVIEW

The election of Republican Abraham Lincoln in November of 1860
led directly to the disintegration of the Union and civil war. After
Lincoln's condemnation of the southern insurrectionists and his call to
arms, thousands of northern black men sought to enlist to serve the
cause of liberation. Their service, however, was spurned. The aim of the
war, averred Mr. Lincoln, was to preserve the Union, not to destroy
slavery. If blacks were permitted to enlist, then a majority of voters
from the border states still in the Union--Maryland, Missouri, Delaware
and Kentucky, as well as anti-abolitionists in the north-- might perceive
abolitionism to be the northern war aim. The support or neutrality of
these people the Union could ill afford to lose. Yet at the same time the
Union could not destroy the Confederacy without the contributions of
African Americans. Only gradually did Lincoln appear to grasp this,
and only gradually did emancipation become fully intertwined with
preservation of the Union as the Northern war objective.

The millions of southern slaves grasped immediately that the war
was about slavery and its eradication. Despite vacillating and ambigu-
ous Union racial policies, they escaped by the thousands and quickly
demonstrated their value to the Union. Each slave lost to the South both
weakened the Confederacy and potentially strengthened the forces of
Union. Union generals such as Benjamin Butler, Davis Hunter, and
Rufus Saxton understood this and exploited the potential of both
"contrabands" and free blacks, who were permitted, at the end of 1862,
to enlist in "Negro regiments". By the end of the war nearly a million escaped slaves had served the causes of Union and freedom. Approximately 180,000 black men served as soldiers for the Union. Of that
number nearly 40,000 perished.

As a necessary wartime measure, President Lincoln issued the
Emancipation Proclamation on January 1, 1863. This not only induced
slave escapes and black recruitment, but it also confirmed the revolu-

tionary social dimension of the Civil War. At stake after January 1863 was the destruction of plantation oligarchy and the system of rigid black oppression upon which it was based. At stake for African Americans were the blessings of liberty.

This liberty, however, would prove elusive to black Americans. Despite the enormity of their war contributions, and incontrovertible proof of their valor and sacrifice, black troops faced discrimination in pay, duties, and opportunity. Their families suffered countless acts of discrimination and deprivation. Promises of just treatment were repeatedly made and broken by agents of the victorious Union government.

REVIEW QUESTIONS

Chapter Content Review

1. Why was Lincoln unable to profess in 1861 that the government's objective in fighting the war was to eliminate slavery?

2. What prevented blacks from enlisting in the Union forces at the start of the war?

3. Who determined the policy for dealing with runaway slaves in the early years of the war?

4. What circumstances contributed to the appalling conditions of the camps for former slaves during the war?

5. Who was responsible for the many initial efforts in black education during the Civil War?

6. From what part of the country were the first black regiments drawn?

7. For what reasons were white Northern laborers particularly upset by the government's policies during the Civil War?

8. By what route did Lincoln attempt to emancipate the slaves of the border states during the Civil War? Why was he unsuccessful?

9. What was the reaction of the "Peace Democrats" to the Emancipation Proclamation?

10. Explain how the Emancipation Proclamation affected the slaves of America?

11. What military and diplomatic benefits did the United States derive from issuing the Emancipation Proclamation?

12. In what ways was the presence of slaves in the Confederacy a source of grave concern for whites?

13. How did the advance of Union troops affect slave behavior?

14. What types of contributions did slaves make to the Confederate war effort?

15. What positions did Jefferson Davis and Robert E. Lee take on the enlistment of slaves?

16. Approximately how many blacks served in the Union Army during the Civil War?

17. Why was the mortality for black Union troops significantly higher than the rate for whites?

18. In what way was the Confederate surrender of 1865 a victory for the South?

Identification Questions

You should be able to describe the following key terms, concepts, individuals and places, and explain their significance:

1. Benjamin F. Butler
2. "contraband of war"
3. American Missionary Association
4. New York draft riots
5. Emancipation Proclamation
6. "running the Negroes"
7. Fifty-fourth Massachusetts Regiment
8. Robert G. Shaw
9. Fort Pillow affair

Essay Questions

1. While Lincoln is viewed by many as being the "Great Emancipator", he was greatly despised by abolitionists across the nation from 1861-1865. Explain why.

2. Why did popular prejudices toward blacks frequently collapse during the Civil War?

SELF-TEST

Multiple Choice

1. Abraham Lincoln:
   a. favored total and immediate emancipation of slaves
   b. supported unconditional abolition without compensation to owners
   c. wanted gradual emancipation with compensation to owners
   d. opposed the idea of colonization of freed slaves outside the United States

2. The Emancipation Proclamation:
   a. represented the first official action taken with regard to slaves
   b. liberated slaves in all slaveholding states
   c. was enthusiastically received by northern whites
   d. was justified as "a fit and necessary war measure"

3. When black men first offered their service as soldiers to the Union, they:
   a. were permitted to enlist, but their pay was less than that of whites
   b. had to sign up for the duration of the war
   c. were rejected
   d. were accepted, but assigned to all black units

Fill in the Blank

4. Four slave states remained loyal to the Union after 1861, Kentucky, Delaware, Missouri, and _____.

5. The _____ passed by Congress in 1861 was the first official step taken to provide "uniform treatment" for fugitives who had taken refuge behind Union lines.

6. _____ was the high ranking Union officer who activated the short-lived "First South Carolina Volunteer Regiment" in 1862.

7. _____ This military unit served a year without pay rather than accept the discriminatory wages at first paid to black soldiers.

True/False

8. Lincoln felt that the war was justified as a means to preserve the Union.

9. Blacks eventually saw military action in every theater of the war.

10. From the beginning, black soldiers received the same treatment that their white counterparts received.

Chapter XII

The Effort to Attain Peace

KEY EVENTS

1863	Lincoln's Ten Percent Plan announced
1864	Congress enacts the Wade-Davis Bill
1865	Freedmen's Bureau established
	Thirteenth Amendment enacted
1867	Reconstruction Act of 1867 enacted
	Congressional Reconstruction commences
1868	Fourteenth Amendment is ratified
1870	Fifteenth Amendment is ratified

CHAPTER OVERVIEW

The Civil War concluded in the spring of 1865. The ravages of that war would be felt well into the 20th century. Millions of people in the war-torn South were destitute, homeless, and hungry. The productive capacity of the region declined to a fraction of its 1860 level. Southern property losses ran well into the billions. There remained little Southern banking of which to speak. Most troubling, however, was the labor transformation of the south. The Civil War destroyed the basis of the southern labor system by eradicating chattel slavery. Emancipation also threw southern social institutions into complete disarray. Politically, the war shattered the rule of the planter oligarchs and left the South in chaos. Finally, the war unleashed the forces of industrial capitalism in the North and paved the way for the domination of the nation by northern capitalists and their Republican allies.

Within this context, the program of Abraham Lincoln and then, after Lincoln's murder, that of his successor, Andrew Johnson, were first tried. Lincoln's plan encouraged rapid Southern restoration to the Union and Johnson accepted the framework of Lincoln's plan. However, after Johnson acquiesced in both the re-empowerment of the secessionist leaders and the enactment of state black codes, Congress repudiated presidential Reconstruction and imposed its own plan. Led by the Radical Republicans, Congress passed and secured (over Johnson's vetoes) the Civil Rights Act of 1866, an extension and expansion of the Freedmen's Bureau, the Reconstruction Act of 1867, and eventually the Fourteenth and Fifteenth Amendments to the Constitution.

The endeavors of the legislatures elected in ex-Confederate states after 1867 to establish peace and prosperity were genuine if not frequently successful. These "radical" state legislatures were composed primarily of southern unionists, northern "carpet-baggers," and African Americans. They approved large expenditures to boost internal improvements, rebuild war damaged areas, and further public education. These state governments demonstrated amply the abilities of African Americans to hold public office responsibly and to serve their constituents effectively. Moreover, black politicians from the South were sent to the United States House of Representatives and the Senate for the first time in American history. In sum, Radical Reconstruction provided the context within which black Americans could participate in and benefit from the democratic order of America.

REVIEW QUESTIONS

Chapter Content Review

1. What factors contributed to the rapid pace of northern industrialization during the war?

2. What immediate economic problems confronted the South after the Civil War?

3. What dangers existed in reuniting the Southern states to the Union?

4. What barriers prevented the nation from resolving a multitude of problems in 1865?

5. What were the provisions of President Andrew Johnson's reconstruction plans?

6. What groups in 1865 merged to oppose Johnsonian Reconstruction? What motivated the opposition of each group?

7. What actions taken by President Andrew Johnson in 1866 won him the bitter enmity of Congress?

8. What were the functions of the Freedmen's Bureau? Why did white southerners and white northerners object to its existence?

9. In what area did the Freedmen's Bureau have the greatest success?

10. Why was the growth of black churches so important to both Reconstruction and the future of black institutions?

11. What prevented the former slaves from achieving enduring economic freedom in the South?

12. What factors militated against cooperation between black and white urban workers in the United States after the Civil War?

13. What obstacles prevented blacks from achieving many successes in starting businesses after the Civil War?

14. What type of blacks typically served in the state legislatures of the South during Reconstruction?

15. What improvements were made in the Southern state governments during Reconstruction?

16. What type of power did black legislators usually wield in the Southern State assemblies after the Civil War?

17. What issues were most significant to the American public and American politicians after 1870?

18. Why did the nation's industrialists seek the end of Reconstruction after 1870?

19. How did Reconstruction lay the foundation for more democratic living in the South? What did the failure of Reconstruction to provide economic security for the former slaves ultimately mean to the South?

Identification Questions

You should be able to describe the following key terms, concepts, individuals and places, and explain their significance:

1. Lincoln's One-tenth (10%) Plan
2. Wade-Davis Bill
3. Black Codes
4. Thaddeus Stevens
5. Freedmen's Bureau
6. Reconstruction Act of 1867
7. Fourteenth Amendment
8. Oliver O. Howard
9. Southern Homestead Act of 1866
10. Freedmen's Bank
11. Hiram Revels
12. Blanche K. Bruce
13. Fifteenth Amendment

Essay Questions

1. In what ways did the political turmoil of the post Civil War years adversely affect the freedmen?

2. In what ways were the late nineteenth century American industrialists responsible for the failure of the former slaves to win economic independence in the south.

SELF-TEST

Multiple Choice

1. With regard to former slaves, the Freedmen's Bureau did all of the following except:
   a. provide them all with 40 acres of land and a mule
   b. furnish supplies and medical service
   c. supervise work contracts between former slaves and employers
   d. establish schools

2. An early blunder committed by the South was the:
    a. repeal of the Black Codes
    b. creation of the Freedman's Bureau
    c. rejection of the Fourteenth Amendment
    d. strong opposition to President Johnson's policies

3. Lincoln's "Ten Percent Plan:"
    a. granted citizenship to ten percent of the former slaves
    b. was designed to restore control in the South to high former Confederate officeholders
    c. had the same provisions as the Wade-Davis Bill
    d. offered amnesty to many southerners

Fill in the Blank

4. The _____ Amendment to the Constitution prohibited slavery in the U.S.

5. The _____ were southern state laws passed after the civil war which severely restricted the civil and political rights of the former slaves.

6. The _____ was the federal protective and welfare agency established by Congress in March of 1865 to aid and guide the former slaves in their transition from slavery to freedom.

True/False

7. Reconstruction is best understood as the period of African-American rule in the postwar South.

8. During Reconstruction, after 1867, black men held public office in the southern states.

9. The Freedmen's Bureau was hindered in its task by southern hostility and inefficiency among its own officials.

10. The largest number of African Americans elected to the U.S. House of Representatives was sent by South Carolina.

Chapter XIII

Losing the Peace

KEY EVENTS

1866 Knights of the Ku Klux Klan formed

1871 Congress repeals the "iron-clad" oath provision of the Reconstruction Act

1873 Panic of 1873

1875 Civil Rights Act barring discrimination in public places and on public carriers enacted Tennessee enacts the first "Jim Crow" law

1876 Compromise of 1876: Reconstruction ends

1883 Supreme Court overturns the Civil Rights Act of 1875

1886 Colored Farmers's National Alliance and Cooperative Union formed

1896 Plessy v. Ferguson

CHAPTER OVERVIEW

Congressional or "Radical" Reconstruction was hated from the outset by most white southerners. To them, Radical or "black" Reconstruction subjected the South to the rule of blacks and "negro-loving

Yankees who encouraged African Americans in the belief that they were equal to whites. Largely excluded from voting in the immediate aftermath of the Civil War, these white southerners observed their legislatures filled with scalawags, carpetbaggers, and, much to their horror, African Americans. Not surprisingly, southern whites did little to cooperate with the "radical" governments. In fact, numerous white supremacist and paramilitary organizations formed in response to "Black Republicanism," and these groups precluded the creation of both stable economic institutions and a harmonious society.

Southern social instability interfered considerably with the designs of Northern industrialists who were anxious to exploit the South's natural resources and to integrate the region into the northern industrial economy. Once northern businessmen, who constituted an important base of Republican power, conceded southern local rule as the price of economic integration, Reconstruction came to a close.

The Compromise of 1876, which ended the period of Reconstruction, was remarkably similar to the Compromises of 1820 and 1850, insofar as each came heavily at the expense of African Americans. Both before and after 1876, southern blacks witnessed the elimination of the Republican Party in the South. As cotton prices plunged and the economic lot of southern whites worsened, both racist demagoguery and the movement to consign blacks to an inferior position in society spread. After the collapse of the populist revolt in 1896, the movement for complete disenfranchisement of blacks helped unite the white South. And from this unity emerged the system of Jim Crow or legalized segregation that pervaded the South into the 1960s. Sanctioned by the United States Supreme Court, codified racial segregation would serve as the cornerstone of the Southern political order emerging at the start of the twentieth century.

REVIEW QUESTIONS

Chapter Content Review

1. What rhetoric were Republicans quick to employ when speaking of their Democratic rivals?

2. Why did Republicans seek to extend the suffrage to the freed-men?

3. What organizations formed during Johnsonian Reconstruction to intimidate both former slaves and Republican sympathizers alike? What was the goal of such groups as the Knights of the White Carmelia and the Ku Klux Klan?

4. Why was the struggle waged in the South from 1865 to 1877 essentially a political struggle?

5. What steps did Congress take beginning in 1869 to restore Southern home rule?

6. Describe the methods employed by white Democrats to oust Radical rule in Louisiana, South Carolina, and Mississippi?

7. Why was the Republican presidential victory in 1876 a victory for Southern Democrats?

8. What tactics, other than intimidation and terror, did Southern Democrats employ to restrict or control black suffrage?

9. What economic forces undermined white unity in the 1880s and 1890s?

10. How did the Populist challenge to Democratic power affect black voting in the South?

11. What lessons did the Democrats and white populists learn about black suffrage in the 1890s? In consequence, what did they agree to do?

12. How did Mississippi disenfranchise blacks in 1890?

13. What impact did the disenfranchisement laws have on Louisiana and Alabama at the start of the twentieth century?

14. What was the cost to the South for maintaining a rigid white supremacist society?

Identification Questions

You should be able to describe the following key terms, concepts, individuals and places, and explain their significance:

1. Union League of America
2. Knights of the Ku Klux Klan
3. *United States v. Cruikshank*
4. Patrons of Husbandry
5. Colored Farmers's National Alliance and Cooperative Union
6. Tom Watson
7. Populist Party
8. poll tax
9. literacy test
10. "grandfather clause"
11. white primaries
12. *Plessy v. Ferguson*, 1896

Essay Questions

1. Discuss the reasons for the decline of Radical Reconstruction, 1869-1876.

2. While having virtually no political power in the South after 1896, Southern blacks were the major focus of all southern state politics. Explain this paradox.

SELF-TEST

Multiple Choice

1. To understand the politics of the Reconstruction period, the student should become familiar with:
   a. the determination of the Republicans to strengthen their position and perpetuate their power
   b. the pressure of industrialists for favorable legislation
   c. conflicting philosophies of Reconstruction
   d. all of the above

2. In the movement to disenfranchise blacks completely through legal means, the South used as prerequisites to voting:
   a. the "grandfather clause"
   b. payment of a poll tax
   c. the ability to read or interpret the Constitution
   d. all of the above

3. Which one of the following did not support the Republican postwar goal of building a strong southern wing of the party?
   a. the Freedmen's Bureau officials
   b. the Knights of the White Camelia
   c. the Union League of America
   d. missionary groups and teachers from the North

Fill in the Blank

4. _____. In the late nineteenth century the southern wing of this political group/party of farmers supported, for a brief time, the right of black men to vote.

5. _____ A protective and benevolent, but most importantly, a political organization, this was the most active agency in the recruitment of blacks in the postwar South for the Republican party.

6. Two of the three states of the former Confederacy that remained   under   Republican   control   in   1876   were
   _____ and _____ .

True/False

7. By 1876 the North had grow weary of the crusade for blacks
   in the South.

8. The movement for disfranchisment of blacks was aided by the
   use of intimidation and violence.

9. One of the results of Radical Reconstruction was the eventual
   emergence of the "solid South."

10. Decisions of the United States Supreme Court had the effect of
    postponing the overthrow of Radical Reconstruction.

Chapter XIV

Philanthropy and Self-Help

KEY EVENTS

CHAPTER OVERVIEW

At the end of Reconstruction southern whites seemed more tolerant of educational institutions for blacks than of any of the other agencies African Americans established in order to improve themselves. The pursuit of education, therefore, came to be one of the greatest preoccupations of blacks, and knowledge was viewed by many as the greatest single opportunity to escape the increasing proscriptions and indignities that whites were heaping on blacks.

Between 1880 and 1930, supporters of black education debated whether African Americans should receive limited education, or a special amount or kind of education, or have access to all the forms of education and training available to white Americans. Among African Americans the most significant exchange regarding these options took place between Booker T. Washington and W. E. B. Du Bois.

Coincident with the growth of black schools in the South was the appearance of philanthropic educational foundations, established for the most part by wealthy white Americans. These agencies did much to broaden the concept of education for blacks in the South and to successfully stimulate self-help on the part of the individual, the institution, and the states of the South.

During a period of American history characterized by sharply declining economic, political, and social opportunities for non-whites, African Americans were convinced that they had to rely chiefly on themselves. As a consequence, they expended enormous energy and creativity in their efforts to make a living and to meet the economic, educational, and social service needs of their race.

REVIEW QUESTIONS

Chapter Content Review

1. What institutions replaced the Freedman's Bureau as the primary supporter of black schools in the South after Reconstruction?

2. What educational aid foundations worked directly to advance the cause of black education in the United States?

3. How did the objectives of church-sponsored philanthropy and of educational foundation philanthropy differ?

4. Did Northern philanthropists advocate the cause of black civil rights in the South?

5. In what ways did Southern blacks contribute to the growth and financial stability of their educational institutions?

6. By what means did Booker T. Washington believe blacks in the South would achieve success?

7. Why was Washington's emphasis on industrial or vocational education acceptable to both southern whites and most people throughout the North?

8. Why was Washington himself regarded so highly by white leaders?

9. What criticism did W.E.B. Du Bois make regarding Booker T. Washington's emphasis on black vocational training and his de-emphasis on civil and political rights for blacks?

10. What criticisms does your textbook make of B.T. Washington's ideas?

11. What factors made it difficult for blacks to purchase farms after the Civil War?

12. By what means did white southerners attempt to restrict the ability of Southern blacks to migrate north or west?

13. Why was life in the southern urban centers both frustrating and unattractive to southern blacks after Reconstruction?

14. To what degree did blacks succeed in participating in the life of nation labor organizations? Explain.

15. Why did businesses both owned and operated by blacks emerge in large numbers throughout urban areas of America during the late nineteenth and early twentieth centuries?

16. What influence did better educated and more progressive black church members have over the direction of their religious communities?

17. In what ways did the black churches promote both education and social improvements?

Identification Questions

You should be able to describe the following key terms, concepts, individuals and places, and explain their significance:

1. Freedman's Aid Society
2. George Peabody
3. John F. Slater
4. John D. Rockefeller
5. Anna T. Jeanes
6. Jubilee Singers
7. Booker T. Washington
8. Tuskeegee Institute
9. doctrine of industrial education
10. W.E.B. Du Bois
11. Jan E. Matzelinger
12. Elijah McCoy
13. Afro-American League
14. T. Thomas Fortune
15. American Negro Academy
16. *Up From Slavery* (1890)
17. *The Colored Cadet at West Point* (1889)
18. George Washington Williams
19. Charles Chesnutt
20. Paul Laurence Dunbar

Essay Questions

1. Compare and contrast the philosophies of Booker T. Washington and W.E.B. Du Bois. To what extent was Du Bois's criticism of industrial education valid? To what extent was it invalid?

2. Black "self-help" took numerous forms after the Civil War. Explain why self-help, vis-à-vis governmental assistance, was necessary, and discuss several of the most successful and beneficial self-help efforts devised by African Americans at this time.

SELF-TEST

Multiple Choice

1. Which of the following people provided substantial financial assistance for the education of southern blacks?
   a. John F. Slater
   b. George Peabody
   c. Anna T. Jeanes
   d. all of the above

2. Booker T. Washington and W.E.B. DuBois:
   a. shared identical philosophies regarding the advancement of African Americans
   b. both expressed disinterest in political and civil rights for blacks
   c. were in agreement as to the type of education blacks most needed
   d. both advocated programs of racial advancement

3. One basic reason why large numbers of African Americans did not become a permanent part of the organized labor movement was that:
   a. most were too lazy to work
   b. since the majority of black workers were skilled, they could make more money outside of the unions
   c. most white workers were prejudiced against black workers and sought to exclude them
   d. black laborers chose to remain aloof

Fill in the Blank

4. _____ This leader opposed the exodus of blacks from the South on the grounds that the government should protect citizens wherever they lived.

5. _____ This labor union, which placed little emphasis on skills, was the only one that made black workers welcome as members.

6. _____ was the author of *The Suppression of the African Slave Trade*, the first scientific historical monograph written by a black man.

True/False

7. Philanthropists contributed substantially to the improvement of education for African Americans in the South.

8. Philanthropists did much to encourage the equitable distribution of tax money for educating all southern youth.

9. The doctrine of vocational education for the black masses met with the general disapproval of most whites.

10. All black leaders agreed that it was desirable for blacks to leave the south and seek work elsewhere.

Chapter XV

Race and the Nation

KEY EVENTS

1867	United States purchases Alaska
1898	Spanish-American War
	Annexation of Hawaii
1899	American occupation of the Philippines begins
1903	American acquisition of the Panama Canal zone
1905	Niagara Movement begins
1906	Brownsville, Texas riot
1908	Springfield, Illinois riot
1909	Formation of NAACP
1911	Formation of the National Urban League
1916	United States lands marines in Santa Domingo
1917	U.S. places Haiti under military rule
	America purchases the Virgin Islands from Denmark

CHAPTER OVERVIEW

For the United States, two of the most far-reaching consequences of Reconstruction and the economic revolution that accompanied it were the end of national isolation and the pursuit of imperialism. America's victory in the Spanish-American war was the major event that transformed the United States into a full-fledged imperial power. It was ironic that African-American soldiers, themselves subject to racist restrictions and viewed as inferiors by most white Americans, should have played a part in bringing extensive numbers of other nonwhites under the domination of the United States. Unlike other imperial powers, however, the United States had a "color problem" at home and therefore had to pursue in its colonies a policy with regard to race that would not upset its segregationist racial policy at home.

Coincident with the rise of the city in American life was the appearance of the African-American ghetto within the city. Though drawn to the cities just as other Americans were for increased economic opportunities, blacks experienced residential segregation, difficulty in securing anything except the most onerous and least attractive jobs, and violent attacks from whites, who viewed them as invaders of their living and employment spaces. The most strenuous efforts to address these problems came from the National Association for the Advancement of Colored People (NAACP) and the National Urban League.

REVIEW QUESTIONS

Chapter Content Review

1. What factors contributed to the United States' growing interest in world affairs after the Civil War?

2. When America declared war on Spain in 1898 most black Americans were anxious to assist their nation in liberating the Cuban people. What views were expressed by the anti-imperialist blacks of America?

3. What two wars did the blacks troops of America face in 1898?

4. To what extent were the famed "Rough-riders" under Teddy Roosevelt indebted to the Ninth and Tenth (Colored) Cavalry units?

5. What racial considerations made the U.S. Congress reluctant to grant full political rights to Caribbean and Latin American peoples at the turn of the century?

6. Explain the means by which the United States forced Haiti and Santo Domingo into its sphere.

7. In which African nation did the U.S. extend its "dollar diplomacy" in the first quarter of the twentieth century?

8. What did President Roosevelt's dinner with Booker T. Washington signify to Southern whites? What did President Roosevelt's dinner with Booker T. Washington signify to African Americans?

9. What difficulties arose when blacks in the early 1900s migrated to cities?

10. One "muckraker" from the ranks of the progressives, Ray Stannard Baker, discussed the "Negro problem" in his book, *Following the Color Line*. What was his solution to the "problem?"

11. How did Teddy Roosevelt's action taken in response to the Brownsville, Texas incident of 1906 ultimately discredit him in the eyes of African Americans?

12. Why were the race riots at the start of the twentieth century so disillusioning and threatening to American blacks? In what way did they refute Booker T. Washington's theories ?

13. In what way did W.E.B. Du Bois, John Dewey, Jane Addams and other progressives respond to these riots?

Identification Questions

You should be able to describe the following key terms, concepts, individuals and places, and explain their significance:

1. Quintin Bandera
2. Colonel James H. Young
3. Emilio Aguinaldo
4. William Hastie
5. William D. Crum
6. Niagara Movement
7. NAACP
8. *Crisis*
9. National Urban League
10. *Guinn v. United States* (1915)
11. *Buchanan v. Warley* (1917)
12. *Moore v. Dempsey* (1923)

Essay Questions

1. While American imperialism adversely affected a multitude of non-white peoples around the world, African Americans played a substantial role in American imperialist ventures. Explain.

2. Explain why "self-help" and private philanthropy were at best only partial solutions to the problems confronting American blacks at the beginning of the twentieth century.

SELF-TEST

Multiple Choice

1. Term applied to the black soldiers by Spaniards in the Spanish-American War.
   a. Black Thunderbolts
   b. Smoked Yankees
   c. Muckrakers
   d. Butchers

2. United States imperialism included annexing all of the following except:
   a. Hawaii
   b. Formosa
   c. the Philippines
   d. Puerto Rico

3. As president, Theodore Roosevelt pleased African Americans when he:
   a. dined with Booker T. Washington
   b. appointed a black man to the collectorship of the Port of New Orleans
   c. refused to accept the forced resignation of the black postmistress at Indianola, Mississippi
   d. all of the above

Fill in the Blank

4. _____ This West Pointer was the only black commissioned officer in the country at the outbreak of the Spanish-American War.

5. _____ was the leader of the Niagara Movement and the first editor of the Crisis, published by the NAACP.

6. The _____ successfully widened opportunities for blacks in industrial employment and in helping black people to solve problems peculiar to the cities.

True/False

7. During the first quarter of the twentieth century some municipalities gave official sanction to the practice of residential segregation.

8. Coincident with the rise of the American city was the rise of the black community within the city.

9. It was in Africa that the United States pursued its new imperialistic policy most vigorously.

10. At the outbreak of the Spanish-American War there were no African-American units in the regular army.

Chapter XVI

In Pursuit of Democracy

KEY EVENTS

1912   Woodrow Wilson elected

1913   Wilson issues executive order segregating black federal workers

1914   World War I begins

1915   Booker T. Washington dies

1917   United States declares war on the Central powers

1918   World War I ends

CHAPTER OVERVIEW

Although African Americans felt extremely discouraged by the increase in segregation during the first years of Woodrow Wilson's presidency, the entrance of the United States into World War I stimulated them to express their patriotism by volunteering for military service in large numbers, through support of wartime emergency measures, and by generous purchase of war bonds. Most hoped that these expressions of devotion to their country would strengthen the claims of minorities to equal rights and undermine segregation. While sizable numbers of African Americans served in the United States Army at home and abroad, segregation remained intact and numerous blacks wearing the uniform of their country were objects of hostility and violence from whites.

American domestic mobilization for the First World War had profound consequences for the African-American community. The expansion of American industries, coupled with the shortage of white native and immigrant laborers, created numerous employment opportunities for African Americans. These opportunities intensified the migration of southern blacks to northern urban centers, causing thousands of African Americans to enter America's cities in search of greater economic, political, and social freedom. These burgeoning black communities increasing came into conflict with surrounding and unwelcoming white neighbors.

REVIEW QUESTIONS

Chapter Content Review

1. Why did African Americans reject the candidacy of Teddy Roosevelt and his Bull Moose Party in the election of 1912?

2. Why did much of the legislation proposed in Congress in 1915 dismay black Americans?

3. How did the U.S. Congress and the nation's military recruitment offices respond to attempts by blacks to serve their nation either as common soldiers or officers?

4. Why was the process of training black regiments so problematic for the War Department?

5. What was the War Department's solution to the problem encountered when the townsfolk of Spartanburg, South Carolina precipitated a controversy with the black Fifteenth New York Infantry ?

6. What contributions did black stevedores make in the war effort?

7. Were the African-American regiments who fought with the French in 1918 major contributors in the war effort? Explain.

8. What tactics did the German army employ in attempting to weaken the efforts of African Americans to subdue them? Did they succeed?

9. How were the African-American troops treated by the French citizens?

10. In what ways did African Americans express their commitment to the war effort?

11. What forces induced hundreds of thousands of blacks to migrate from the South during the War?

12. Why would white Southerners create numerous obstacles to black migration?

13. What role did the National Urban League play in the process of black migration?

Identification Questions

You should be able to describe the following key terms, concepts, individuals and places, and explain their significance:

1. *Birth of a Nation*
2. Emmett J. Scott
3. stevedore regiments
4. 369th United States Infantry
5. Henry Johnson
6. Pan African Congress (1919)
7. *Secret Information Concerning Black Troops*
8. A. Philip Randolph
9. Chandler Owen
10. *The Messenger*

Essay Questions

1. Discuss the various types of discrimination practiced against American blacks both immediately prior to and during World War I, and explain various reasons why African Americans would, despite their mistreatment, enlist in the military and support the war effort so fervently.

2. Ironically, at the same time that Americans fought to "make the world safe for democracy," democracy was being undermined in the United States. Explain.

SELF-TEST

Multiple Choice

1. As president, Woodrow Wilson by executive order:
    a. segregated black federal employees in eating and rest room facilities
    b. phased out most blacks from the civil service
    c. did both of the above
    d. did neither of the above

2. The movie *Birth of a Nation*
    a. glorified black manhood
    b. told a positive and accurate story of black emancipation
    c. was blatantly anti-black
    d. received little, if any, attention from the public

3. During World War I blacks were barred entirely from the
    a. cavalry
    b. marines
    c. engineer corps
    d. stevedores

Fill in the Blank

4. _____ This black U.S. infantry regiment was called "hell Fighters" by the Germans and for their bravery won the French <u>Croix de Guerre.</u>

5. _____ This black newspaper, published in New York by A. Philip Randolph and Chandler Owen, refused to support the war effort as almost all other black publications did.

6. _____ was appointed special assistant to the Secretary of War and served him as confidential advisor on matters relating to the African Americans.

7. _____ Term given to the sensational feat of a black private in helping to repulse a German raiding party in May 1918.

True/False

8. There was a surprising lack of friction between American white southerners and African-American soldiers during the war.

9. The first black servicemen to arrive in Europe were combat troops.

10. The black press, for the most part, supported the war with enthusiasm.

Chapter XVII

Democracy Escapes

KEY EVENTS

1916   Knights of the Ku Klux Klan grow to more than 100,000

1918-1919   Return and demobilization of African-American servicemen after World War I

1919   Outbreak of race riots and other expressions of racial strife occurs

The NAACP begins effort to secure passage of a federal anti-lynching law

George Baker, known as "Father Divine," founds an interracial religious community that addresses the practical and spiritual needs of some African Americans

1916-1920   Marcus Garvey establishes the Universal Negro Improvement Association (UNIA) as part of the first mass movement among African Americans

1919   The Commission on Interracial Cooperation established

1923   U. S. Congress fails to pass a federal anti-lynching bill

1925   Marcus Garvey enters a United States federal prison to begin serving a five year sentence for mail fraud

1927   Marcus Garvey pardoned and deported by President Calvin Coolidge

CHAPTER OVERVIEW

Black American veterans of World War I were welcomed home enthusiastically by their communities. They were also confronted by the Ku Klux Klan, whose resurgence reflected powerful sentiments among white Americans for the preservation of white supremacy and a deep resentment at the expanded black presence in America's cities and in jobs previously "for whites only." These tensions resulted in race riots that produced numerous black and white injuries and deaths, as well as considerable destruction of property.

In the African-American community there were several responses to these conditions: the NAACP increased both its demands for black equality and its efforts to secure passage of a federal anti-lynching law in the United States Congress; Marcus Garvey and his black nationalist movement received widespread support from the black masses; and various black religious communities that promoted separatism and self-help grew in influence and numbers.

REVIEW QUESTIONS

Chapter Content Review

1. How did African-American soldiers who served abroad in World War I feel at the end of the war about returning to the United States?

2. What was the Ku Klux Klan? What were its major beliefs and goals?

3. What was a lynching? By whom were African Americans lynched in the aftermath of World War I? And why?

4. Why did James Weldon Johnson, the executive secretary of the NAACP, call the summer of 1919 "the red summer?"

5. What were the causes and the consequences of the race riot in Chicago in July 1919? Why was it considered the most serious race riot that year?

6. In what way was the willingness of African-American riot victims to retaliate in their own defense a new factor in American race relations? What were the causes of this new behavior on the part of blacks? Why did some white Americans believe that "foreign influences" were responsible for African Americans' new assertiveness?

7. Who was Claude McKay? And how did he contribute to greater understanding of new attitudes among African Americans?

8. What steps did the NAACP take to seek protection for African Americans in the aftermath of World War I? Were the efforts of the NAACP successful?

9. Who were the founders of the Commission on Interracial Cooperation (CIC)? What kind of work did it begin following World War I? How successful was the CIC?

10. Who was Marcus Garvey? Why did his organization grow so rapidly in the United States? What were the major beliefs and goals of the Garvey movement?

11. Was Garvey's movement a success or failure? And why?

12. Who was Father Divine? And what kind of message and programs did he offer the African American masses?

13. Were the message and programs of Father Divine helpful or harmful to American blacks? Explain.

Identification Questions

You should be able to describe the following key terms, concepts, individuals and places, and explain their significance:

1. Ninety-second Division
2. Peace Mission
3. Dr. O. H. Sweet
4. Representative L. C. Dyer
5. Black Star Line
6. *Thirty Years of Lynching in the United States, 1889-1918*

Essay Questions

1. Why did white Americans fight in World War I to make the world "safe for democracy," and, at the conclusion of the war, refuse to grant equal rights to its African American citizens?

2. Why do you think so many African Americans believed the ideas and programs of Marcus Garvey were the answer to their problems? Were Garvey's ideas correct and his solutions to problems practical?

3. Compare the post-World War I activities of the NAACP to promote the well-being of African Americans with the efforts of the UNIA to do the same thing. Which of the two organizations was more effective? Why?

SELF-TEST

Multiple Choice

1. Which of the following most accurately describes the Ku Klux Klan of the post war years?
   a. Unlike the first Klan, it welcomed black members
   b. It was a racist, reactionary, white supremacist organization
   c. Its membership was confined to the South
   d. It condemned violence as a means of achieving its objectives

2. An epidemic of race riots, beginning n the summer of this year, led to its designation as the "Red Summer:"
   a. 1919
   b. 1920
   c. 1929
   d. 1930

3. In the case of *Smith v. Allwright*, the United States Supreme Court held that:
   a. the grandfather clause violated the Constitution
   b. residential segregation ordinances were unconstitutional
   c. each state must provide integrated educational opportunities for all citizens
   d. the exclusion of blacks from the Democratic primary was a violation of the Fifteenth Amendment.

Fill in the Blank

4. _____ was the term applied to the summer of 1919 because of the intensity and widespread nature of racial strife then.

5. _____ was the name of the black nationalist organization founded by the "Black Moses."

6. The most successful black union of the postwar period, founded by A. Philip Randolph, was _____.

7. _____ was the racist, reactionary white supremacist organization that was revived in 1915 and flourished in the United States in the 1920s.

True/False

8. Most black soldiers who served in France refused to return to the United States after the war.

9. Hindering the work of the NAACP was its policy of excluding whites from membership.

10. In the first signs of recession in the mid-1920s, large numbers of blacks lost their jobs.

Chapter
XVIII

The Harlem Renaissance and the Politics of African American Culture

KEY EVENTS

1920   Charles Gilpin in title role of *Emperor Jones*

1921   Opening of *Shuffle Along*

         Claude McKay, *Harlem Shadows*

1923   Jean Toomer, *Cane*

         Opening of *Liza*; *Running' Wild*; and *Chocolate Dandies*

1924   Jessie Redmond Fauset, *There is Confusion*

         Paul Robeson in *All God's Chillun Got Wings*

1925   Countee Cullen, *Color*

         Alain Locke, editor, "Harlem Number", *Survey Graphic*

1926	Langston Hughes, *Weary Blues*
1927	Opening of *Porgy*
1928	Nella Larsen: *Quicksand*
1929	Jessie Redmond Fauset, *Plum Bun*
1932	Sterling Brown, *Southern Road*
1934	Zora Neale Hurston, *Jonah's Gourd Vine*
1937	Zora Neale Hurston, *Their Eyes Were Watching God*

CHAPTER OVERVIEW

Following World War I, the work of leading white American intellectuals and artists reflected a shift toward realism and social consciousness. This stimulated an interest in African Americans in the arts that helped to create a receptive climate for the work of creative blacks in some influential and affluent segments of the white community. The outpouring of African American artistic activity in the 1920s and 1930s, centered in (but not exclusive to) New York City's Harlem, was described at various times as the "Harlem Renaissance," or the "Black Renaissance," or the "New Negro Movement."

The unifying theme in the varied creative activity of black novelists, short story writers, poets, painters, sculptors, filmmakers, dancers, singers, actors, art critics, and other contributors was their use of their talents to confront the racism and unfairness that shaped the black experience in an America controlled by whites.

REVIEW QUESTIONS

Chapter Content Review

1. Why did a number of white writers become interested in the American race problem following World War I?

2. Name three of these white writers and list the works they produced that reflected this interest.

3. What were the two important developments in the African American community during and immediately after World War I that fostered the growth of the New Negro Movement?

4. What African American community became most closely identified with the New Negro Movement? In what city was it located? And why did it come to be so closely associated with the movement?

5. List five of the major literary contributors to the Black Renaissance, including at least two women, and indicate their most important works.

6. Who were some of the actors and performers that expressed the spirit of the Black Renaissance in plays and musicals?

7. List the names and major works of several painters or sculptors who were a part of the New Negro Movement of the 1920s and 1930s.

8. What African American communities in Southern and mid-Western cities became significant centers of the Black Renaissance?

9. Who were the people Zora Neale Hurston described as "Negrotarians?" And what did she mean by this term?

10. Were all the African American writers associated with the New Negro Movement "crusaders?" If some were not, what was their artistic motivation?

11. Who was probably the most prolific of the writers that contributed to the Black Renaissance?

12. What were the titles and who were the stars of some of the best-known and most popular black musical revues during the 1920s?

13. Describe the independent black film movement of the 1920s. And indicate the ways in which the New Negro Movement influenced the black independent film movement.

14. Name three jazz artists who were part of the Harlem Renaissance and list their contributions.

Identification Questions

You should be able to describe the following key terms, concepts, individuals and places, and explain their significance:

1. Moorfield Story, *Problems of Today*
2. "Yet do I marvel at this curious thing/ To Make a poet black, and bid him sing"
3. *The Green Pastures*
4. F.E. Miller, Aubrey Lyle, Eubie Blake, and Noble Sissle
5. Florence Mills
6. Roland Hayes
7. *The Banjo Lesson*
8. Zora Neale Hurston.

Essay Questions

1. Discuss the ways in which the growing interest of white Americans in social issues during the post-World War I period set the stage for the Black Renaissance.

2. Analyze how and why the African American community in New York City became the most important cultural center in black America.

3. Were black women as much participants in the New Negro Movement as black males? If so, why do you think this was so? If not, why not?

SELF-TEST

Multiple Choice

1. The Harlem Renaissance produced a talented assemblage of Black:
   a. professional basketball players
   b. New York politicians
   c. business leaders
   d. writers

2. A widely acclaimed singer who, on one occasion sang from the steps of the Lincoln Memorial when the Daughters of the American Revolution denied her the use of Constitution Hall in Washington, was:
   a. Marian Anderson
   b. Leontyne Price
   c. Camilla Williams
   d. Jessye Norman

3. Which of the following was responsible for producing the black writers who contributed to the Harlem Renaissance:
   a. The desire to stimulate the use of black English
   b. An attempt to produce literary works for an all-black audience.
   c. A keener realization of injustice and the improvement of the capacity for expression.
   d. The desire to embrace and to publicize the doctrines of socialists and communists.

Fill in the Blank

4. _____ and were two publications, one of the Urban League and the other of the NAACP, that were among the first to open their pages to black poets.

5. _____ was a brilliant black musical revue that opened in New York City in the summer of 1921.

6. _____ Many students of the period contend that the Harlem Renaissance ended with this production which appeared in 1930.

True/False

7. The literature of the Harlem Renaissance was, for the most part, remarkably free of race consciousness.

8. Even before the twenties, New York City had become the intellectual and cultural center of black America.

9. Before the 1920s came to an end, the creative forces of the Harlem Renaissance made themselves felt throughout the entire African American community in the United States.

10. Awareness of the gap between the American promise of freedom and their own experiences made African Americans bitter and defiant.

Chapter XIX

The New Deal

KEY EVENTS

1925 Brotherhood of Sleeping Car Porters and Maids established

1928 Oscar DePriest of Chicago, a black Republican, elected to the U. S. House of Representatives

1929 Stock market crashes; "Great Depression" begins

1930 Nomination of John J. Parker to U. S. Supreme Court receives strong opposition from the African American community; Parker fails to win Senate approval

1931 The "Jobs For Negroes" movement began in St. Louis

1932 Angelo Herndon, a black member of the Communist Party, is arrested, tried, convicted, and sentenced to 18 years in prison on the charge of inciting to insurrection

The nine "Scottsboro boys" are arrested on charges of rape

1933 The Citizens League For Fair Play organized in New York City

1934 Arthur W. Mitchell of Chicago, a black Democrat, defeats Oscar DePriest for reelection

1935   African Americans riot in New York City

1935-1936 John L. Lewis establishes the Congress of Industrial
               Organizations (CIO)

1936   Majority of African Americans desert the Republicans
               and vote Democratic in presidential election

CHAPTER OVERVIEW

The desperate need of American blacks for economic relief during the
Great Depression was expressed in self-help campaigns such as the
"Jobs For Negroes" movement and the Citizens League For Fair Play.
During the 1920s and increasingly in the 1930s, blacks began to involve
themselves with the organized labor movement, despite widespread dis-
crimination in most unions.

During these same years, more African Americans voted in local
and national elections, making possible an increase in the number of
black elected officials, including the election of the first black members
of Congress since the end of Reconstruction. The New Deal programs
of Franklin D. Roosevelt, however, and the activities of Eleanor Roosevelt and other liberal white New Dealers caused the majority of African
Americans to shift from the Republican to the Democratic Party.

REVIEW QUESTIONS

Chapter Content Review

1. What new areas of employment did African Americans enter in
   the decade following World War I?

2. What was the most significant step in the 1920s toward the
   unionization of African Americans?

3. What were the most important types of businesses in the African American community in the two decades after World War I?

4. Did the situation of black American farmers improve or worsen from 1920 to 1940?

5. Once the Great Depression began, how were African Americans treated in the administration of relief services?

6. What were causes of the political resurgence in the African American community from 1920-1940?

7. Why did many black voters begin to desert the Republican party during the 1920s?

8. What was the name and party of the African American elected to the United States House of Representatives in 1928? What made it possible for him to win election?

9. Were African Americans strong supporters of the bid of Franklin D. Roosevelt for the U.S. presidency in 1932?

10. Was the Communist Party attractive to African Americans?

11. How did African Americans view Eleanor Roosevelt? And why?

12. What was the name and party of the African American elected to the United States House of Representatives in 1934? What made it possible for him to win election?

13. What was President Franklin D. Roosevelt's "Black Cabinet?" Who were some of its members? And what were their responsibilities?

14. Which New Deal agencies were most beneficial to the interests of African Americans?

15. What were the causes of the Harlem riot of 1935?

16. How did John L. Lewis and the CIO make labor unions attractive to black workers?

Identification Questions

You should be able to describe the following key terms, concepts, individuals and places, and explain their significance:

1. Friends of Negro Freedom
2. National Association For the Promotion of Labor Unionism
3. *Messenger*
4. American Negro Labor Congress
5. Angelo Herndon
6. John J. Parker
7. United Front Against Fascism
8. Harold L. Ickes
9. Reverend John H. Johnson

Essay Questions

1. Discuss the history of the establishment of the Brotherhood of Sleeping Car Porters and Maids and explain why the creation of this labor union had such great significance for African Americans.

2. Describe the life of a black cotton or tobacco farmer in the South during the 1920s and 1930s and explain why his/her economic situation declined during these years.

3. Explain why African Americans employed in the automobile and the food processing industries of the North were affected so immediately and so negatively at the onset of the Great Depression in 1929.

SELF-TEST

Multiple Choice

1. Three of the following are true of Oscar DePriest. Which one
   is **not** true?
   a. His first elective office was that of Chicago alderman
   b. He was elected to Congress in 1928
   c. He was the first black Democrat ever to sit in Congress
   d. His presence in Washington symbolized the regeneration
   of black Americans in politics

2. Roosevelt's black advisors differed from earlier black presidential advisors in which of the following important respects?
   a. Their number was larger
   b. They served in significant official positions
   c. They were highly trained persons entrusted with specific
   functions to perform
   d. All of the above

3. All of the following are reasons why many southern white
   leaders found the New Deal distasteful except:
   a. It concentrated too much power in Washington, D.C.
   b. Its relief and recovery programs were administered
   directly from Washington, D.C., with no implementation
   on the local level.
   c. It relieved the suffering of many of those on whose
   poverty some white politicians had climbed to power.
   d. It undertook to force equality in the administration of its
   benefits

4. One reason why Franklin D. Roosevelt succeeded in gaining a large following among blacks was that:
   a. He refused to tolerate discrimination in the administration of New Deal relief programs.
   b. He dined with Booker T. Washington in the White House
   c. Blacks came to regard New Deal economic programs as especially beneficial to them
   d. He established a "Negro Bureau" designed to deal with all matters affecting black people.

Fill in the Blank

5. These nine young African-American men were unjustly arrested on rape charges in 1932 and their subsequent conviction became a rallying point for civil rights advocates. _____.

6. This man founded the Congress of Industrial Organizations (CIO) and led efforts to extend unionization and union benefits to African Americans. _____.

7. This man was both the founder of the Brotherhood of Sleeping Car Porters and Maids and co-publisher of the *Messenger*. _____.

True/False

8. Oscar DePriest was the first black Democrat ever to sit in the United States Congress.

9. The Great Depression hit the black wage earner with particular severity.

10. From its beginning, the CIO sought to organize workers regardless of race or skill.

Chapter XX

The American Dilemma

KEY EVENTS

1870 Illiteracy rate for African Americans above ten years old is 81%

1899 Supreme Court renders decision in *Cumming v. The School Board of Richmond County, Ga.*

1900 By this year every state in the South enacts laws that provide for separate schools for blacks and whites

In 1900 for every $2 spent on the education of blacks in the South, $3 was spent on whites

1916 The Association for the Study of Negro Life and History begins publication of the *Journal of Negro History*

1929-1941 Depression causes special hardships for Southern schools for African Americans

1930 Illiteracy rate for African Americans above ten years old drops to 16%

1935 Donald Murray, an African American, wins his suit for admission to the University of Maryland Law School

1936 National Negro Congress founded

1937   Southern Negro Youth Congress founded

1939   On Easter Sunday Marian Anderson, the great con-
tralto, performs on the steps of the Lincoln Memorial

Hattie McDaniel wins an Oscar for her role in *Gone
With The Wind*

1943   Thirty-three historically black institutions of higher
education form the United Negro College Fund

1944   Black and white Southerners establish the Southern
Regional Council

American Council on Race Relations founded

1949   Ada Sipuel, an African American, wins her suit for
admission to the University of Oklahoma Law School

1952   Ralph Ellison's *Invisible Man* wins the National Book
Award

1954   On May 17 the U. S. Supreme Court outlaws segregation in its *Brown v. The Board of Education* decision

1965   Malcolm X assassinated

1968   Martin Luther King, Jr. assassinated

1970   By this year there are 378,000 African Americans in
predominantly white colleges and universities

1977   By this year there are 1.1 million African Americans in
predominantly white colleges and universities, account-
ing for 9.3 per cent of the nationwide enrollment that
year

1984   By this year the number of African Americans attending institutions of higher education had dropped to 993,574; of these, 267,000 were in historically black institutions, which continued to provide more than half of all the bachelors' degrees received by African Americans

CHAPTER OVERVIEW

During the twentieth century African Americans expressed an intense desire for access to all levels of education, public and private. Their educational progress could be seen in the following: steadily rising rates of school attendance; dramatic increases in literacy; expansion in the number of historically black educational institutions and the programs they offered; a series of legal victories for African Americans in the South who sued for admission to historically white educational institutions; expanded access to libraries and organizations such as the Young Men's Christian Association, the Young Women's Christian Association, the Boy Scouts, and the Girl Scouts; a visible growth in the number of highly trained African American professionals; the establishment of several influential scholarly journals within the black community; the expanding readership of black newspapers and popular magazines; the growing membership, influence, and wealth of many black religious communities; the establishment of several new and influential black and interracial organizations committed to promoting equal rights and racial harmony; scholarly studies by highly respected scholars that began to challenge citizens of the United States to face and resolve the "American Dilemma;" new community and educational programs that sought to address the needs of minority youth; and, most important of all, the historic 1954 decision of the United States Supreme Court outlawing segregation of schools in *Brown v. Board of Education*.

Twentieth century impediments to the progress of African Americans included: flagrantly discriminatory underfunding of black education in the South; frequently segregated and often inadequate schools for blacks in the South, North and West; limited opportunities in most fields of employment and areas of opportunity for all but the most talented and gifted of African Americans; the widespread refusal of many white Americans, especially those in Southern states, to comply with the *Brown v. Board of Education* decision; and the destructive impact of negative conditions in urban environments on black individuals and their families.

Numerous talented young African Americans emerged as major figures in music--most notably in jazz, gospel, the concert stage, and opera--and in literature as novelists, short story writers, poets, play-wrights, and critics. Black American actors, however, would have only the most limited access to the increasingly influential and highly lucra-tive medium of movies, where they were usually cast in stereotyped ra-cial roles.

REVIEW QUESTIONS

Chapter Content Review

1. What was the decision of the United States Supreme Court in *Cumming v. The School Board of Richmond County, Ga.?* When was the decision handed down? And how did it affect African Americans?

2. Who was Ambrose Caliver? And what was his impact on the African American community?

3. What were the three "general-types" of historically black col-leges?

4. Who was the first African American to gain admission to the University of Maryland Law School? And on what grounds did the court decree admission?

5. What were the specifics in the United States Supreme Court's decision in *Missouri ex rel. Gaines v. Canada, Registrar of the University et al.?* When was the decision delivered?

6. What important strategic decision did the NAACP make in 1951 in regard to its campaign for equal rights for African Americans?

7. Name some of the scholarly journals established by African Americans and historically black colleges and universities during the 20th century.

8. List some of the cities in which jazz flourished during the 20th century? Who were some of the outstanding musicians in this field?

9. To whom is the success and popularity of gospel music during the 1930s and later largely attributed?

10. What were the events that led to a concert by Marian Anderson on the steps of the Lincoln Memorial on Easter Sunday 1939?

11. Who were Margaret Walker and Gwendolyn Brooks? And what did they have in common?

12. What were the subjects of Richard Wright's books? And why is he considered to be such an important writer?

13. What was the Nation of Islam? And what role did it play in twentieth African American history?

14. Why did African Americans invest so much time and energy in their religious institutions? What were some of the tangible signs of the importance of churches to blacks? Why were African Americans so little interested in integrating their churches?

15. Why did the number of black newspapers and magazines increase rapidly after World War I?

16. What were the goals of the National Negro Congress and the Southern Negro Youth Congress? In what kinds of public activities did they engage to promote those goals?

17. What were the goals and activities of the Southern Conference for Human Welfare? And how did it seek to promote the well-being of the African American community?

18. In what part of the United States was the American Council on Race Relations active? What were its goals and activities?

19. Explain the differences and similarities in the following organizations and their programs: Operation Headstart; Higher Horizon; SEEK; and Access To Excellence.

Identification Questions

You should be able to describe the following key terms, concepts, individuals and places, and explain their significance:

1. Atlanta University System
2. United Negro College Fund
3. Marguerite Ross Barnett
4. Ada Sipuel
5. Ella Fitzgerald & Lena Horne
6. "Precious Lord, Take Hand"
7. *Invisible Man*
8. *The Fire Next Time*
9. Malcolm X
10. National Negro Association
11. *Ebony, Jet, Tuesday,* and *Monitor*
12. Negro History Week
13. William Grant Still
14. Leontyne Price
15. James Baldwin
16. Ralph Ellison
17. Hattie McDaniel
18. Gunnar Myrdal

Essay Questions

1. Trace the history of the various legal decisions that made education more accessible to African Americans.

2. Discuss the ways in which the shift of many African Americans from the rural South to America's urban centers led to the creation of blacks' separate world within the cities of the United States.

3. Examine the conclusions of Gunnar Myrdal's 1944 study, *An American Dilemma*, and discuss whether they are still relevant or now irrelevant to black-white relations in 20th century America.

SELF-TEST

Multiple Choice

1. Certain trends in the higher education of blacks became noticeable in the second half of the twentieth century. Which of these was **not** one of them?
    a. A dramatic increase in the enrollment of blacks in predominantly white colleges and universities.
    b. A marked increase in the number of black administrators in black colleges.
    c. Graduate and professional training of blacks decreased noticeably.
    d. The number of black administrators in predominantly white colleges increased.

2. *Brown v. Board of Education* was concerned with:
    a. equal rights for women.
    b. voting rights for black people.
    c. discrimination in the sale of housing.
    d. racial segregation in public schools.

3. By 1900, every state in the South had enacted laws that provided for:
   a. free tuition grants to blacks enrolled in graduate programs in the region's public universities.
   b. separate black and white public schools.
   c. admission of qualified black students to the predominantly white professional schools of the section.
   d. a system of integrated elementary schools.

Fill in the Blank

4. _____ was the founder of the Association for the Study of Negro Life and History.

5. _____ wrote the decision in the *Brown v. Board of Education* case.

6. _____ This foundation assisted in the construction of more than five thousand school buildings for African Americans in fifteen states between 1913 and 1922.

True/False

7. In the twentieth century, the interest of blacks in education noticeably declined.

8. African Americans obtained court support for their entrance into hitherto all-white southern graduate and professional schools.

9. Protests of African Americans against their status reflected a lack of pride in their race and its history.

10. James Baldwin and Richard Wright were two of the most prominent African-American musicians of the 1940s and 1950s.

Chapter XXI

Fighting For The Four Freedoms

KEY EVENTS

1935 Italy invades Ethiopia

1936 African American Olympic medalists Jesse Owens and Ralph Metcalfe insulted by Hitler in Berlin

1939 World War II begins with Hitler's invasion of Poland

1940 In September black American leaders submit a seven-point program to President Roosevelt outlining minimum essentials for giving African Americans just consideration in the defense program

    In October, Colonel B. O. Davis becomes the first African American to be promoted to the rank of brigadier-general

1941 In January A. Philip Randolph advocates march on Washington

    In June, President Roosevelt issues Executive Order 8802 banning discrimination in defense industries

On December 7 the Japanese attack Pearl Harbor; Doris Miller, a black Navy messman, shoots down four enemy planes

1942   Approximately 370,000 African American men enter the armed services

1943   On June 20 the most serious domestic race riot of the World War II years began in Detroit

1944   On July 8 the War Department issues order forbidding racial segregation in its recreational and transportation facilities

1945   World War II ends; approximately one million African American men and women served in the U.S. Armed Forces during its duration

1950   Ralph Bunche becomes the first African American to receive the Nobel Peace Prize for his work as a United Nations mediator in Palestine

CHAPTER OVERVIEW

In the years leading up to the start of World War II, African Americans recognized that some of the world's most racist and anti-democratic forces were represented in the rise of fascism and nazism. From 1939, when the United States began to shift from an official position of neutrality to one of military preparedness and active support of the Allied Powers, to the close of World War II in 1945, blacks in America fought continuously for access to the various branches of the Armed Services, for the right to be trained and commissioned as officers, for equal and non-discriminatory services in the military, and, equally important, for jobs in government agencies and employment sectors receiving federal funding. African Americans' greatest success in regard to fair employment came in 1941 when President Roosevelt issued Executive Order 8802 in response to the threat of a national demonstration by blacks against racism in the United States.

Although African Americans fought in segregated military units in World War II, their numbers steadily increased and their treatment by whites in the services improved over the course of the war. When blacks received greater respect and better treatment, it was almost always the result of their outstanding military performance. Nevertheless, during the war years there were numerous incidents of violence against black males and females in the service.

On the home front, there were numerous racial clashes as African Americans entered defense plants and communities where their presence was resented. For African Americans World War II constituted a fight against oppression at home as well as abroad. When the conflict ended with the structure of Jim Crow segregation still intact in their country, black leaders turned to the newly formed United Nations as their best hope for help in fighting the forces of American racial prejudice.

REVIEW QUESTIONS

Chapter Content Review

1. How many African Americans served in the United States Army in 1940 and what were some of their units?

2. Did the Selective Service Act of 1940 initially promote the entrance of African Americans into the United States Army?

3. In September 1940 what requests did African American leaders make of President Roosevelt?

4. Who was A. Philip Randolph and what was the "March On Washington" plan he conceived in January 1941? How was the plan received by African Americans and the Roosevelt administration. Did the plan produce any results?

5. What were the "Four Freedoms" to which President Roosevelt frequently made reference as America's wartime goals? What do you think were the differences and similarities in how black and white Americans understood the "Four Freedoms" to apply to their lives?

6. What were the events that made it possible for African Americans to serve as fighter pilots in World War II?

7. What were the events that made it possible for African Americans to serve as officers in the United States Navy?

8. When were officers candidate schools opened to African Americans? What was the rate of graduation of blacks from these schools? And were these officer candidates schools segregated?

9. Why did the World War II service of the all black Ninety-second Division become so controversial?

10. Why was it so difficult to maintain high morale among African Americans in the military services?

11. Who was Doris Miller? And what services did he render for his country during World War II?

12. What were some of the major industries in which African Americans gained employment during World War II?

13. What were some of the distinct ways that African-American women supported the American war effort in the military services and on the home front?

14. Why did so many African Americans migrate to the North and West during World War II?

15. What was the date and the cause of the Detroit race riot during World War II?

Identification Questions

You should be able to describe the following key terms, concepts, individuals and places, and explain their significance:

1. Ethiopia
2. Executive Order 8802
3. 761st Tank Battalion
4. Ninety-ninth Pursuit Squadron
5. Captain Hugh Mulzac
6. Private George Watson
7. Crystal Bird Fauset
8. Dr. Charles Drew
9. Ted Poston
10. *Negroes and the War*
11. United Nations
12. Jan Smuts
13. Ralph Bunche
14. Charles H. Houston

Essay Questions

1. Trace the history of the "March on Washington" movement led by A. Philip Randolph.

2. Choose any branch of the United States Armed Forces that existed between 1940-1945 and do a history of the service of African-American men or women or both in that branch.

3. Do a history of the 1943 race riot in Detroit.

SELF-TEST

Multiple Choice

1. During World War II, blacks for the first time were permitted
   to serve in the:
   a. Marine Corps
   b. infantry
   c. signal corps
   d. field artillery

2. The most serious riot of the World War II period occurred in:
   a. Los Angeles
   b. Atlanta
   c. Detroit
   d. New York

3. Director of the United Nation's Trusteeship Council, he was
   winner of the Nobel Peace Prize in 1950:
   a. W. E. B. Du Bois
   b. E. Franklin Frazier
   c. Walter White
   d. Ralph Bunche

Fill in the Blank

4. _____'s threat to organize a massive protest march on
   Washington, D.C. forced President Roosevelt to issue an executive order forbidding racial discrimination in employment in
   defense industries.

5. The famous executive order referred to in number one above
   was called _____.

6. _____ was the first African American to obtain the
   rank of brigadier general in America's armed forces.

7. _____ Organized in San Francisco in 1945, this international body is committed to the settlement of world problems and the maintenance of peace among nations.

True/False

8. Because it did not directly affect them, African Americans failed to condemn the fascist movement in Europe.

9. Job discrimination in the defense industry was eliminated by the Committee on Fair Employment Practices.

10. The "Double-V" campaign stood for victory over the Germans as well as over the Japanese.

Chapter XXII

African Americans in the Cold War Era

KEY EVENTS

1946	Harry S Truman appoints presidential commission on civil rights which issues the report, *To Secure These Rights*
1947	Jackie Robinson signed by the Brooklyn Dodgers as the first African-American player in major-league baseball
1948	Harry S Truman appoints presidential commission on race relations in the armed forces which issued the report, *Freedom To Serve*
	President Truman issues an executive order forbidding discrimination in the hiring policies of the federal government
	The U. S. Supreme Court outlaws restrictive covenants
1949	Following the recommendations of *Freedom To Serve*, the United States began to integrate its armed forces
1950-1951	United States' forces fighting in the Korean War becomes first integrated American army in U.S. history

1950   The U.S. Supreme Court rules that segregation of African Americans on dining cars of interstate railroads is illegal

Professional basketball and tennis integrated with the admission of African-American players to teams and tournaments

1952   A majority of African-American voters supported the losing Democratic candidate, Adlai Stevenson, in the presidential election

1953   E. Frederick Morrow appointed administrative assistant in the executive offices of the president of the United States

1954   Three African Americans, all Democrats, elected to the United States House of Representatives

1955   The Interstate Commerce Commission decrees all racial segregation on interstate trains and buses must end January 10, 1956

Near Greenwood, Mississippi Emmett Till, a fourteen year old African American, is murdered for allegedly whistling at a white woman

1956   The African-American communities of Montgomery, Alabama and Tallahassee, Florida begin a boycott of their respective city bus lines to secure better treatment and services for black patrons

The governors of South Carolina, Georgia, Mississippi, and Virginia call on Southern states to declare that the federal government has no power to prohibit segregation and to protest the "encroachment" of the federal government on the "sovereignty" of the states

Ninety Southern members of Congress issue their "declaration of constitutional principals," commonly known as the "Southern Manifesto" Several Southern states pass laws to stop the operation of the NAACP within their borders.

A federal court orders the State of Alabama to admit Autherine Lucy, an African-American applicant, to the University of Alabama

Nat "King" Cole, an African-American singer, briefly hosts his own television show

1963   Sidney Poitier, an African American, wins Oscar as best actor for his performance in *Lilies of the Field*

1964   Six African Americans elected to the United States House of Representatives

1965   Carl Rowan, an African American, begins to write a syndicated column and to appear on national radio and television as a commentator

1966   Bill Cosby, an African American, receives an Emmy Award for his role in the television series "I Spy"

1968   The Congress passes the Fair Housing Act barring racial discrimination in the sale, rental, or financing of most housing units

1970   A sharp rise in the number of black female-headed families begins--an indication of the pressures weakening the African-American family

Maya Angelou, *I Know Why The Caged Bird Sings*

1970-1974   During these years the "Flip Wilson Show," the first variety show hosted by an African American, was consistently rated among the top programs on television

1974   Max Robinson, an African American, became a national anchorman for the "ABC Evening News"

1976   Ntozake Shange, *For Colored Girls Who Have Considered Suicide/When The Rainbow Is Enuf*

1977   Millions of American viewers see Alex Haley's "Roots," a television mini-series

1978   James A. McPherson's *Elbow Room* won the Pulitzer Prize for fiction

The boxer Muhammad Ali (Cassius Clay) once again wins crown as world heavyweight champion. He lost the title several years earlier when he was found guilty of violation of the Selective Service Act

1980   Robert L. Johnson establishes the Black Entertainment Network (BET) as part of the cable television system

1982   Alice Walker's *The Color Purple* receives the Pulitzer Prize

1983   By this year some 48 per cent of all black children under 18 live in female-headed households

Bryant Gumbel selected to co-host NBC's "Today Show"

1985   Oprah Winfrey begins her television program, "The Oprah Winfrey Show"

1986   Spike Lee, *She's Gotta Have It*

Charlayne Hunter-Gault becomes a regular correspondent on MacNeil-Lehrer News Hour

1988   Toni Morrison's *Beloved* won the Pulitzer Prize

1989   Bernard Shaw becomes principal anchor in Washington, D.C. for the Cable News Network (CNN)

1992   Spike Lee, *Malcolm X*

1993   Rita Dove becomes the youngest U. S. poet laureate

William A. Hilliard, editor of the *Portland Oregonian*, elected as first black president of the American Society of Newspaper Editors

Bob Herbert joins the *New York Times* as the first African-American columnist on its Opinion and Editorial Page

CHAPTER OVERVIEW

During the three decades after World War II, the general situation of the African-American community steadily improved, economically, politically, and socially. Blacks, their hopes and ambitions stimulated by the vision of freedom proclaimed in wartime propaganda, pressed both individually and through their racial institutions, to push the doors of equality and opportunity ever wider. Their successful efforts were assisted frequently by strategic support from a broad range of predominately white organizations committed to reforming race relations in the United States. The courts, chiefly but not exclusively the federal ones, increasingly took cognizance of racial questions and frequently ruled in favor of equality. The executive branch of the federal government, moreover, sensitive to both domestic and foreign pressures, exerted considerable influence in eradicating the gap between creed and practice in America.

The improvement of the status of African Americans, however, was neither uniform nor without vigorous opposition in some quarters. In the Southern states, African Americans faced white resistance to integration in the form of economic reprisals, violence from officers of the law as well as from extra-legal vigilante groups, and public political opposition from the majority of elected officials in the region. Parts of the

South saw the amount of violence rose to proportions of a reign of terror.

Throughout the United States, responsible citizens, concerned about mounting racial tension, called for federal action, but neither the president nor the Congress seemed inclined to intervene. One of the most dramatic facts of life for black Americans in the Cold War Era was their continuing urbanization. This was directly responsible for many of the positive changes above, particularly the growing political strength of African-American voters, and the willingness of the two major political parties to court those voters by rhetorical and sometimes actual support of efforts to secure equal rights for blacks.

There were, however, significant negative aspects to urbanization. In many instances, the arrival of blacks in the central cities of the United States caused whites to depart, taking with them the majority of employment opportunities that blacks sought. The black ghetto that had become a fixture in urban America earlier in the twentieth century gained a measure of permanence during the black migration of the World War II and postwar years, as most blacks found it very nearly impossible to purchase or rent in predominantly white communities. Perhaps the most troubling development was the dramatic deterioration of the black family, most graphically reflected in the sharp rise in the number of African-American female-headed households beginning in the 1960s and accelerating in the 1970s.

By contrast, those African Americans who benefited most from expanded opportunities made possible the revitalization and expansion of black religious institutions, the growth in circulation and influence of black newspapers and magazines, and the expanded presence of blacks in various new and old businesses that serviced the African-American community and in predominantly white business enterprises. For Americans of all races, expanded opportunity for African Americans was demonstrated by the fame and, in some instances, the large financial rewards that came to those talented blacks whose achievements made them prominent in literature, the arts, music, journalism, theatre, films, sports, and television.

REVIEW QUESTIONS

Chapter Content Review

1. What specific actions did President Harry S Truman take to promote equality for African Americans?

2. How did the decisions of courts during the Cold War Era affect the status and treatment of African Americans?

3. During what war did the United States deploy its first integrated army?

4. Who was the first African-American player in major league baseball?

5. Who were the two African Americans elected national officers of the AFL-CIO in 1955? And what was the importance of this event?

6. What was the name of the fourteen year old African American killed in Mississippi in 1955? And what was the alleged cause of his murder?

7. In what two cities did African Americans begin a boycott of the city bus lines to secure better treatment and service for black patrons? And what year did the boycotts begin?

8. What was the "Southern Manifesto?"

9. Who was the first African American to host his own television show?

10. Who was the first African-American male to win an Academy award for his performance in a film?

11. Who was the author of book on which the television mini-series "Roots" was based? And what are the subjects of the book and mini-series?

12. By 1980 did the majority of African Americans live in urban or rural areas? What were the percentages?

13. Who is Robert L. Johnson? And what is his major achievement in the television industry?

14. When did observers begin to notice the rise within the African-American community of female-headed families? And why was this so troubling?

Identification Questions

You should be able to describe the following key terms, concepts, individuals and places, and explain their significance:

1. *Freedom To Serve*
2. Autherine Lucy
3. "The Flip Wilson Show"
4. Muhammad Ali (Cassius Clay)
5. *The Color Purple*
6. Bryant Gumbel
7. "The Oprah Winfrey Show"
8. Rita Dove
9. William Hilliard
10. Highlander Folk School
11. Chicago *Defender*
12. North Carolina Mutual Life Insurance Company
13. Elizabeth Catlett
14. Andre Watts
15. Wynton Marsalis
16. *She's Gotta Have it*
17. "Amos and Andy"

Essay Questions

1. Trace the history of Harry S Truman's support of black civil rights while in the White House. Discuss how he became interested in civil rights and what the ultimate goals of his civil rights policies were.

2. Present a history of the integration of African-American players into professional baseball.

3. Present a history of the resistance to racial integration of any one of the Southern states that practiced legal segregation during the Cold War Era.

SELF-TEST

Multiple Choice

1. Which of the following was the last branch of the federal government to move actively in the area of civil rights for Negroes?
    a. the executive
    b. the legislative
    c. the judicial

2. Economic actions invoked against blacks who were active in civil rights in the 1950s included:
    a. dismissals from jobs.
    b. denials of loans.
    c. foreclosures of mortgages.
    d. all of the above.

3. Southern white leaders fought school desegregation in several ways. Which of these was **not** one of them?
    a. turning schools over to private organizations.
    b. encouraging "voluntary segregation."
    c. threatening to secede from the Union.
    d. adopting "freedom of choice" plans.

Fill in the Blank

4. _____ was the name of the presidential report that called for positive programs to strengthen civil rights.

5. _____ and _____ were the two African Americans elected vice-presidents of the labor organization formed by the merger of the AFL and CIO.

6. _____ was the federal district judge who, in 1947, decided that African Americans could not be excluded from the Democratic primary in South Carolina.

True/False

7. President Truman contributed to the creation of a climate in which the status of blacks was officially degraded.

8. A battlefield test of armed forces integration received its first widespread application in Korea.

9. The political influence of African Americans increased substantially in the post-World War II decades.

10. Southern resistance to any change in the status of African Americans often degenerated into violence.

Chapter XXIII

The Black Revolution

KEY EVENTS

1957 Governor Orval Faubus of Arkansas actively opposes the desegregation of Central High School in Little Rock

At President Eisenhower's initiative the Congress passes a civil rights law

1960 On February 1 four students from the North Carolina Agricultural and Technical College in Greensboro conduct the first major civil rights "sit-in" of the decade

By this year there were more than one million registered African-American voters in twelve Southern states; and in at least six of the eight most populous states in the country, blacks held the balance of power in closely contested elections

John F. Kennedy's close victory over Richard M. Nixon in the presidential election is aided greatly by Kennedy's receipt of the majority of the African-American vote

1960-1961 Strong protests in New Rochelle, New York; Englewood, New Jersey; Chester, Pennsylvania; and Chicago, Illinois against school segregation in the North

1961   In May the Congress of Racial Equality (CORE) sends "freedom riders" into the South to test segregation laws and practices in interstate transportation

1962   By this year more than thirty cases had been initiated by U.S. attorney general Robert Kennedy to protect blacks in their efforts to vote in Mississippi, Louisiana, Alabama, Tennessee, and Georgia

In the face of serious opposition and with federal intervention James Meredith is admitted to the University of Mississippi

1963   Governor George Wallace is unable to block the enrollment of an African-American student at the University of Alabama

Medgar Evers, the leader of the Mississippi NAACP, is assassinated outside his home in Jackson

On August 28, 1963, as part of the "March on Washington for Jobs and Freedom", Martin Luther King delivers his "I Have A Dream" speech

On November 22, President Kennedy is assassinated in Dallas

1964   In January the Twenty-Fourth Amendment to the Constitution, outlawing the poll tax, was ratified

In June the Civil Rights Act of 1964 was passed by Congress

Fannie Lou Hamer addresses the Democratic National Convention, as part of an effort to replace the all-white Mississippi delegation with the integrated Mississippi Freedom Democratic party delegation

George Wallace, the segregationist governor of Alabama, makes a strong showing in the presidential primaries of Wisconsin, Indiana, and Maryland

During the summer, major eruptions of racial violence, rioting, and looting occur in New York City, Rochester, Patterson, Elizabeth, and Jersey City, New Jersey; Philadelphia, and Chicago

In November the vast majority of African-American voters cast their ballots for the winning Democratic ticket of Lyndon B. Johnson and Hubert H. Humphrey. California voters adopt by an overwhelming vote a constitutional amendment guaranteeing a property owner the right to dispose of her/his property to anyone he/she chooses. In 1966 the California Supreme Court declares this amendment unconstitutional.

By this year less than 2 percent of the African-American students in the eleven states of the former Confederacy are in desegregated schools.

1965   President Johnson appoints Robert Weaver Secretary of the new Department of Housing and Urban Development, making Weaver the first African American to hold a cabinet office.

Martin Luther King, Jr. receives the Nobel Peace Prize.

In February a young civil rights worker and a young white minister from Boston are killed in Selma, Alabama. To protest these events, Martin Luther King leads an interracial march from Selma to Montgomery. Snipers murder a white woman from Detroit who had participated in the march.

At the urging of President Johnson, Congress passes the Voting Rights Act. In August the predominately black Watts area of Los Angeles erupts in a major race riot.

Malcolm X killed in New York City.

1965-1966   In the eleven Southern states of the former Confederacy six percent of African-American children attended desegregated schools.

1966   Stokely Carmichael, the new chairman of the Student Nonviolent Coordinating Committee (SNCC), urges the use of "black power" to combat "white power."

1967   President Johnson appoints Thurgood Marshall as the first African American to serve on the Supreme Court.

The Black Power Conference in Newark, New Jersey calls for the "partitioning of the United States into two separate independent nations, one to be a homeland for white and the other to be a homeland for black Americans."

A group of young militants in California led by Huey P. Newton and Bobby Seale organize the Black Panther Party

1968   On April 4 Martin Luther King is killed in Memphis. In more than one hundred cities several days of rioting and burning and looting ensued.

By this year 20.3 percent of the African-American schoolchildren in the former Confederate states are in "fully integrated schools."

The report of the National Advisory Commission on Civil Disorders states that "our nation is moving toward two societies, one black, one white--separate and unequal."

1969   The Black Economic Development Conference meets in Detroit and calls upon the "White Christian Churches and the Jewish Synagogues and all other Racist Institutions" to pay $500 million in reparations and to surrender 60 percent of their assets to be used for economic, social, and cultural rehabilitation of the black community."

1971   President Richard M. Nixon warns federal officials to stop pressing for desegregation of Southern schools through "forced busing."

        Shirley Chisholm conducts an unsuccessful campaign for the Democratic presidential nomination.

1973   The National Black Feminist Organization was founded.

1976   More than 90 percent of all black voters support Jimmy Carter, the winning Democratic presidential candidate.

1978   The Supreme Court rules in the *Bakke* case that the factor of race alone could not be used to guarantee the admission of a certain number of blacks to a public medical college in California.

        By this year more than 90 percent of the school systems in the South are classified as desegregated.

1983   Guion S. Bluford becomes the first African-American astronaut.

1992   Mae E. Jemison becomes the first female African-American astronaut

CHAPTER OVERVIEW

Between 1960 and 1980 large numbers of African Americans resorted to direct action in order to secure for themselves the rights of American citizens. The widespread, massive, official and unofficial resistance of whites to the extension of these rights to African Americans was one of the great stimulants to black activism. In many Southern communities economic sanctions were invoked against blacks who were active in civil rights, including dismissals from jobs, denial of loans, and foreclosures of mortgages. When these measures were ineffective, violence, including murder, was frequently employed.

Throughout the United States, but especially in the South, the response of African Americans and their allies to opponents of civil rights and desegregation took the forms of boycotts, political action, sit-ins, voter-registration drives, freedom rides, freedom marches, and lobbying for new laws to guarantee protection of civil rights by the local, state, and federal government. In all these efforts the growing size and political clout of black urban communities, North, South, and West, caused the major political parties to pay attention to black concerns and in some instances to promote them. The efforts of African Americans to secure their rights and the desire of the great majority of Americans for racial peace helped to make possible passage of the Federal Civil Rights Act of 1964 and the Federal Voting Rights Acts of 1965.

As the civil rights movement gained momentum, many of its supporters came to see it not only as an effort to obtain political equality for African Americans, but also as a campaign for black economic equality, particularly in the areas of housing and employment. The inability, however, of the civil rights movement to effectively promote changes in white attitudes and behavior that would guarantee economic equality for the majority of African Americans was directly responsible for the enhanced appeal of the Black Muslims, the Black Power Movement, and the Black Panther Party. The most negative statements of black disappointment and hopelessness in this regard were the urban riots of the 1960s and 1970s. And the belief of numerous female participants in the civil rights movement that the majority of the movement's male leaders were sexist produced some of the earliest forms of individual and organized black feminism.

REVIEW QUESTIONS

Chapter Content Review

1. What states passed fair employment laws between 1945 and 1959?

2. Name the governor of Arkansas who opposed the desegregation of Little Rock's Central High School in 1957.

3. What country became the first former African colony to join the United Nations? And on what date did this occur?

4. In what year did the Greensboro, North Carolina "sit-in" action to promote civil rights for African Americans take place? And who were the individuals that initiated it?

5. In what Northern cities did major protests against school segregation take place in the years 1960 and 1961?

6. What was the name of the organization which sent "freedom riders" into the South in 1961?

7. How far had desegregation of schools in Southern and border states proceeded by 1961?

8. Describe the ruling handed down on September 22, 1961 by the United States Interstate Commerce Commission regarding segregation.

9. What was the content of the executive order issued in 1962 by President John F. Kennedy in regard to discrimination and housing?

10. Who was the first African American admitted to the University of Mississippi? And in what year did the admission take place?

11. Name the governor of Alabama who sought in 1963 to block the admission of an African American to his state's university?

12. Name the leader of the NAACP in Mississippi who was shot outside his home in 1963.

13. What was the date, place, and occasion on which Martin Luther King, Jr. delivered his famous address on civil rights in the United States? What was the title of the address?

14. Name and describe two decisions of the United States Supreme Court in 1963 that strengthened the resolve of civil rights activists.

15. Describe the Twenty-fourth Amendment to the United States Constitution. And give the year it was ratified.

16. Give a general description of the Civil Rights Act of 1964.

17. Who was Fannie Lou Hamer? And what did she attempt to do at the Democratic National Convention in 1964?

18. Who was George Wallace? And what important victories did he achieve in the presidential primaries in 1964?

19. What amendment to the Constitution of the state of California was adopted by voters in 1964? How did the Supreme Court of California treat a challenge to this amendment in 1966?

20. Who was the first African American to be appointed to the presidential cabinet? In what year did the appointment take place? And to what post was this individual appointed?

21. What major international award did Martin Luther King, Jr. receive in 1965?

22. What events promoted a major civil rights march from Selma to Montgomery in the state of Alabama in 1965?

23. Give a general description of the Voting Rights Act of 1965.

24. What major American city experienced a devastating race riot in 1965?

25. Name the black civil rights leader killed in New York City in 1965?

26. How far had the desegregation of Southern schools progressed by 1966?

27. Who became chairman of the Student Nonviolent Coordinating Committee (SNCC) in 1966? And what new tactic did this individual advocate for the promotion of African-American equality?

28. How many African Americans were members of the Congress of the United States in 1966?

29. What new organization to promote African-American equality was founded in 1967? Who were its founders?

30. When and where was Martin Luther King, Jr. killed? And what were the immediate consequences of his death?

31. How far had school desegregation progressed in the Southern states by 1968?

32. What was the demand made by the Black Economic Development Conference on America's all-white and predominantly white religious institutions in 1969?

33. What was the approximate size of the Black Muslim community by the early 1970s?

34. What warning did President Richard M. Nixon issue to federal officials in 1971 concerning the use of busing to promote desegregation of schools?

35. Who was the first African-American woman to campaign for the Democratic presidential nomination? And in what year did she seek it?

36. What presidential candidate did the bulk of African-American voters support in 1976?

37. What was the decision of the United States Supreme Court in the *Bakke* case? And in what year was the decision rendered?

38. What was the level of desegregation in Southern public schools in 1978?

39. Name the major American cities that had African-American mayors in 1979.

40. Name the first African-American male astronaut and the first African-American female astronaut? In what year or years did each take her/his first flight?

41. In what major cities did major race riots occur?

Identification Questions

You should be able to describe the following key terms, concepts, individuals and places, and explain their significance:

1. Orval Faubus
2. Ghana
3. "sit-in"
4. "freedom riders"
5. James Meredith
6. George Wallace
7. Medgar Evers
8. Cambridge, Maryland
9. "I Have A Dream"

10. *Edwards v. South Carolina*
11. *Johnson v. Virginia*
12. Twenty-fourth Amendment
13. Civil Rights Act of 1964
14. Fannie Lou Hamer
15. Council of Federated Organizations
16. Robert Weaver
17. Selma to Montgomery March
18. Voting Rights Act of 1965
19. Watts
20. Malcolm X
21. Stokely Carmichael
22. *United States v. Jefferson County*
23. Black Power Conference of 1967
24. Huey P. Newton and Bobby Seale
25. April 4, 1968
26. National Advisor Commission on Civil Disorders
27. Black Economic Development Conference of
28. Shirley Chisholm
29. Yvonne Braithwaite Burke
30. National Black Organization
31. Barbara Jordan
32. Louis Martin
33. Guion S. Bluford
34. Mae E. Jemison.

Essay Questions

1. Compare and contrast the presidential records of Dwight D. Eisenhower, John F. Kennedy, Lyndon B. Johnson, and Richard M. Nixon in regard to support for equal rights for African Americans.

2. Do a history of the "sit-in" launched in 1960 by the four African-American students at North Carolina Agricultural and Technical College in Greensboro. Be sure to explain why you think they risked their lives and futures in this way.

3. Discuss the differences and similarities in the tactics of Martin Luther King, Jr. and Malcolm X, as well as the influence each had on African Americans and other Americans.

4. Examine the ways in which the Black Power Movement turned the Civil Rights in a new direction. And assess whether the overall impact of the Black Power movement was good or bad.

SELF-TEST

Multiple Choice

1. In 1960 four students from North Carolina Agricultural and Technical University:
    a. inaugurated a back-to-Africa movement.
    b. issued a Black Power manifesto.
    c. declared the South an unfit region for African-Americans.
    d. launched a "sit-in" movement.

2. During his years as president of the United States John F. Kennedy:
    a. secured passage of tough new civil rights laws by the United States Congress.
    b. made no appointments of African Americans to important federal offices.
    c. sought to elevate black Americans through expanded executive action and moral leadership.
    d. refused to take any active role in efforts to secure James Meredith's admission to the University of Mississippi.

3. The Watts riot occurred in the city of:
    a. New Orleans.
    b. Chicago.
    c. Las Vegas.
    d. Los Angeles.

4. The Black Panther Party for Self Defense advocated:
   a. The creation of one or more all-black states in the United States.
   b. non-violence as the chief tactic of the civil rights movement.
   c. Total liberty for black Americans or total destruction for America.

Fill In the Blank

5. _____ This amendment outlawed the requirement of the poll tax, long a means of disenfrachising African Americans in federal elections.

6. _____ Appointed an Associate Justice of the United States Supreme Court, this person was the first African American to occupy a seat on that bench.

7. _____ This kind of segregation, often found in the North, results from the concentration of blacks in certain well-defined geographic areas, rather than from statutory regulation.

True/False

8. President Kennedy's religion made him unacceptable to the vast majority of black voters.

9. The term nonviolence is closely associated with the early years of the Black Revolution.

10. A combination of executive action and federal legislation was successful in preventing the outbreak of racial violence in the mid-sixties.

Chapter XXIV

"New Forms of Activism"

KEY EVENTS

1974   Rap music emerges as a distinctive expression of African American culture

1977   Andrew Young, an African American, appointed United States Ambassador to the United Nations

1980   Ronald Reagan elected president by an enormous majority; 90 percent of the African-American vote goes to the defeated Jimmy Carter

1981   On January 15, 100,000 marchers converge on Washington, D.C. to rally for a national holiday for Martin Luther King, Jr.

By this year AIDS had begun to have a major impact on the African-American community

1982   The African-American unemployment rate was 18.9 percent, more than twice the white rate of 8.4 percent

1983   In October Jesse Jackson announces his candidacy for the Democratic nomination for president

On November 2 President Reagan signs the bill establishing a national holiday in honor of Martin Luther King, Jr.

1984   On Thanksgiving Day four prominent African-American leaders begin a sit-in in the South African Embassy to protest apartheid and the detention of black South African leaders

1985   While the African-American unemployment rate was 16.3 percent, the unemployment rate for whites was 6.2 percent; at the same time the unemployment rate for young blacks (16-19) soars to more than 50 percent for the first time in history

Douglas Wilder elected the first African-American lieutenant-governor of Virginia

1986   The National Black Gay and Lesbian Conference is established

1988   For the second time Jesse Jackson announces his candidacy for the presidential nomination of the Democratic party

George Bush elected president, while 90 percent of the African-American community cast their votes for the losing Democratic candidate, Michael Dukakis

Congress passes an Anti-Drug Abuse Act, leading to the appointment of the first "drug czar"

1989   Douglas Wilder elected the first African-American governor of Virginia

George Bush appoints Colin Powell to the most important military post ever occupied by an African American, Chairman of the Joint Chiefs of Staff

1990   In June Nelson Mandela, one of the most prominent leaders of the black South African liberation movement, makes a twelve day visit to the U.S., during which he addresses a joint session of Congress

1991   Congress authorizes President Bush to use military force against Iraq and to expel it from Kuwait. Every African-American Democrat in Congress votes no

The first democratically elected president of Haiti is ousted: President Bush suspends aid to Haiti and refuses to recognize the new regime

Clarence Thomas is nominated to the United States Supreme Court by President Bush and confirmed by the United States Senate

Earvin "Magic" Johnson and Arthur Ashe announce they were infected with the AIDS virus

In March Rodney King, an African American, is arrested and beaten by police in Los Angeles; the beating is videotaped by a passerby

1992   In March the National Minority AIDS Council accuses federal agencies of providing inadequate financial support to prevent the spread of AIDS among Americans of African, Hispanic, Asian, and Native American ancestry

In April, after the Los Angeles police officers who arrested Rodney King were acquitted of the charge of using "excessive force," Los Angeles erupts into four days of rioting, looting, and burning

In November the Democratic presidential ticket of Bill Clinton and Albert Gore win election; 83 percent of the African-American vote went to Clinton and Gore

Carol Moseley-Braun of Illinois is elected to the U.S. Senate and becomes the first African-American woman to serve in that body

The total number of African Americans in the U.S. House of Representatives reaches thirty-nine

President Clinton chooses four African Americans to serve as cabinet officers.

1993   After the four policemen who arrested Rodney King are tried in federal court for violating King's civil rights, two are found guilty and two acquitted

Toni Morrison awarded Noble Prize for literary achievements.

CHAPTER OVERVIEW

In 1980 Ronald Reagan won the presidency of the United States with an overwhelming victory. Ninety percent of the African-American vote, however, went to his Democratic opponent, James Earl Carter, as it had four years earlier. Whether justified or not, African Americans were deeply distrustful of Reagan's intentions toward them. During the eight years he held office these negative perceptions grew stronger for a number of reasons. Despite Reagan's choice of an African American as secretary of Housing and Urban Development, blacks were disappointed that so few members of their race received appointments. And as the President initiated policies and measures that reflected his goals, most African Americans saw them as evidence that the Reagan administration had little or no commitment to supporting racial diversity in government; was opposed to the implementation of voting rights, school desegregation, equal employment opportunity, and affirmative action; was committed to weakening the force of the Civil Rights Act of 1964 and the Voting Rights Act of 1965; and had little interest in Americans at the lower end of the income scale, especially blacks.

To African Americans the most dramatic symbol of this was President Reagan's begrudging support of the effort to get the United States Congress to approve a national holiday in honor of Martin Luther King, Jr. When President Reagan left the White House in 1988, he was succeeded by George Bush, his former vice-president. To most African

Americans the four years of the Bush administration represented little or no change from the racial policies of the Reagan administration.

For many African Americans the most positive political development of the Reagan-Bush years were the two dramatic and highly publicized, though unsuccessful, campaigns of the African-American leader Jesse Jackson for the Democratic presidential nomination. Few other events seemed to focus the attention of the black community on the value of the political process as a means of bringing their issues and concerns to the attention of the American people. Jackson's action and rhetoric generated hope in an African-American community reeling under the impact of severe unemployment, high levels of illegitimate births to young black females, rising rates of crime and violence, a drug epidemic, inadequate and increasingly ineffective public schools, an AIDS crisis, and numerous expressions of black popular culture that reflected a profound sense of alienation.

In the presidential campaign of 1992, with Jesse Jackson no longer a participant, African-American voters seemed to see in Bill Clinton, the Democratic presidential candidate, and his running mate, Al Gore, an interest in their problems that had not been evident during the Reagan and Bush years. Eighty-three percent of the African Americans who voted in November 1992 supported the victorious Clinton-Gore ticket.

REVIEW QUESTIONS

Chapter Content Review

1. What is Rap music? And what is its message?

2. Who was the first African American ever to become a full general in the United States military?

3. What African-American leader met with the president of Syria and the head of the Palestine Liberation Organization (PLO) in 1979? And for what purpose?

4. Who was the winning presidential candidate in 1980? And what percentage of the African-American vote did he receive?

5. Why did President Reagan withdraw the nomination of William Bell to chair the Equal Employment Opportunity Commission (EEOC)?

6. What were the actions that Jesse Jackson and his organization took to persuade the Coca-Cola Company and other businesses to increase the number of their black employees and expand services to the African-American Community?

7. By what year was AIDS identified as a major public health issue for the African-American community?

8. What was the public response to the Reagan administration's reversal in 1982 of an eleven-year policy in regard to the tax-exempt status of private educational and certain other non-profit institutions?

9. What was the unemployment rate in the African-American community in 1982?

10. Who was the first African-American mayor of Chicago? And when was he elected?

11. What was the cause and result of Jesse Jackson's trip to Syria in 1983?

12. What was the reason that four prominent African-American leaders began a sit-in at the South African embassy in 1984?

13. What was the unemployment rate in the African-American community in 1985?

14. When and for what purposes was the National Black Gay and Lesbian Conference established?

15. Who was the winning presidential candidate in 1988? And for whom did the majority of African-Americans vote?

16. What was the decision of the Supreme Court in the case of *City of Richmond v. J. A. Crosson Company*?

17. When and why did the United States Congress pass an Anti-Drug Abuse Act? And what is a "drug czar?"

18. What message did Jesse Jackson send to the ruler of Panama in 1988? What was the response?

19. Who was the first African American to be elected governor of Virginia? And in what year was he elected?

20. Who was the first African American to be appointed Chairman of the Joint Chiefs of Staff? In what year was he appointed? And by whom was the appointment made?

21. What decisions did the United States Supreme Court render in the cases of *Patterson v. McLean Credit Union, Ward's Cove Packing Company v. Atonio,* and *Martin v. Wilks*? In what year or years were the cases decided? And what was the importance of these cases to African-American history?

22. Why did President Bush veto the Civil Right Bill passed by the United States Congress early in 1990? What caused him to sign, later in the same year, another version of the bill passed by the United States Congress?

23. In what year did the Bush administration issue a directive placing restrictions on "race-specific" scholarships? Why did the administration issue the directive? And why was it withdrawn shortly after being issued?

24. Who was Nelson Mandela? And what was the purpose of his visit to the United States in 1990?

25. Who was the first democratically elected president of Haiti? And what was President Bush's response to his ouster?

26. Who was the African American nominated by President Bush to the United States Supreme Court? In what year did the

nomination take place? What controversies arose in connection with this nomination? And was the nominee confirmed?

27. Name the two African-American athletes who announced in 1991 they were infected with the AIDS virus.

28. Who was Rodney King? When and why was he arrested and beaten by police in Los Angeles?

29. What decision did the United States Court of Appeals deliver concerning Haitian exiles in 1991?

30. What charge did the National Minority AIDS Council make against federal agencies in 1992?

31. What was the cause or causes of the Los Angeles riot of 1992?

32. When and why did Earvin "Magic" Johnson resign from the National Commission on AIDS?

33. What percentage of the African-American vote did the Clinton-Gore ticket receive in the presidential election of 1992?

34. Who was the first African-American woman to be elected to the United States Senate? When was she elected? And what state did she represent?

35. Who was the African-American appointed chair of President-Elect William J. Clinton's transition team?

36. How many African Americans did President Clinton choose to serve in his cabinet? And who were they?

37. What was the outcome of the federal trial of the four Los Angeles police officers accused of violating the civil rights of Rodney King?

38. How many African Americans were members of the United States Congress in 1992?

Identification Questions

You should be able to describe the following key terms, concepts, individuals and places, and explain their significance:

1. Rap music
2. Daniel "Chappie" James
3. Andrew Young
4. William Bell
5. HIV
6. AIDS
7. Harold Washington
8. Robert Goodman
9. apartheid
10. Douglas Wilder
11. National Black Gay and Lesbian
12. *City of Richmond v. J. A. Crosson Company*
13. William Bennett
14. Colin Powell
15. Louis W. Sullivan
16. *Patterson v. McLean Credit Union, Ward's Cove Company v. Atonio,* and *Martin v. Wilks*
17. "race-specific" scholarships
18. Nelson Mandela
19. Clarence Thomas
20. Anita Hill
21. Earvin "Magic" Johnson
22. Arthur Ashe
23. Rodney King
24. National Minority AIDS Council
25. Carol Moseley-Braun
26. Vernon Jordan.

Essay Questions

1. Discuss the race relations policies of the Reagan Administration and the response of the African-American community to them.

2. Trace the history of Jesse Jackson's two campaigns for the presidential nomination of the Democratic Party. What impact did the two Jackson campaigns have on the African-American community and on the United States as a whole.

3. What were the most important ways in which President George Bush and his administration dealt with the black Americans? In what ways did the African Americans communicate their views of President Bush and his racial policies?

SELF-TEST

Multiple Choice

1. The first African American ever to become a four-star general in the United States military was:
   a. Daniel "Chappie" James
   b. Colin Powell
   c. Douglas Wilder
   d. Rodney King

2. Which president of the United States, somewhat reluctantly, signed the bill establishing a national holiday in honor of Martin Luther King, Jr.?
   a. Richard Nixon
   b. Gerald Ford
   c. Jimmy Carter
   d. Ronald Reagan

3. In 1984 Randall Robinson and three other prominent African-American leaders began a sit-in at the embassy of South Africa to protest that nation's policy of apartheid. Who was the South African leader released from prison six years after this protest?
   a. Manuel Noriega
   b. Nelson Mandela
   c. Harold Washington
   d. Jesse Jackson

4. Jesse Jackson was:
   a. the leader of both Trans-Africa and the Department of Housing and Urban Development in the 1980s
   b. the first African American to be appointed United States ambassador to the United Nations
   c. opposed to the bill in Congress that created a national holiday in honor of Martin Luther King, Jr.
   d. a two-time campaigner for the Democratic Party's nomination for President of the United States.

Fill in the Blank

5. _____ One of the two prominent African Americans who disclosed in 1991 that they were infected with AIDS.

6. _____ was the first female African American elected to the Senate of the United States.

7. _____ was the first democratically elected president of Haiti.

True/False

8. President Bill Clinton named only one African American to serve in his cabinet.

9. Rap music originated in the American South during the 1940s and 1950s.

10. Anita Hill, in her testimony before the Senate Judiciary Committee, raised questions about the character of Supreme Court nominee Clarence Thomas.